SASKATCHEWAN HOMESTEAD

Book One

1920-1924.

SEC.23,TP.43,RGE.21,W.2

J. KEN MULLEN

Note for Librarians: A cataloguing record for this book is available from Library and Archives Canada at www.collectionscanada.ca/amicus/index-e.html
ISBN 1-4120-6886-x

Printed in Victoria, BC, Canada. Printed on paper with minimum 30% recycled fibre. Trafford's print shop runs on "green energy" from solar, wind and other environmentally-friendly power sources.

Offices in Canada, USA, Ireland and UK
This book was published *on-demand* in cooperation with Trafford Publishing. On-demand publishing is a unique process and service of making a book available for retail sale to the public taking advantage of on-demand manufacturing and Internet marketing. On-demand publishing includes promotions, retail sales, manufacturing, order fulfilment, accounting and collecting royalties on behalf of the author.

Book sales for North America and international:
Trafford Publishing, 6E–2333 Government St.,
Victoria, BC V8T 4P4 CANADA
phone 250 383 6864 (toll-free 1 888 232 4444)
fax 250 383 6804; email to orders@trafford.com
Book sales in Europe:
Trafford Publishing (UK) Limited, 9 Park End Street, 2nd Floor
Oxford, UK OX1 1HH UNITED KINGDOM
phone 44 (0)1865 722 113 (local rate 0845 230 9601)
facsimile 44 (0)1865 722 868; info.uk@trafford.com
Order online at:
trafford.com/05-1797

10 9 8 7 6 5 4 3 2

Although the J. Mullen family, and many friends actually lived. This novel about them necessitated a few additional characters to fill in the blanks where people probably existed. But have been forgotten. Most of the conversation is made up. Most of the stories took place. This work is dedicated to the real people, relatives, and friends of the Mullen's. Because they left a precious legacy toward the growth of the canadian prairies, and should be remembered.

I have done the best I can to relate the stories that I heard and from the few notes written in a hospital in the last few weeks of John Mullen's life on earth. No offence is meant to anyone. This is just the way I saw their lives unfold as homesteaders.

JKM

MANY PEOPLE CAME
OF EVERY NAME
AND WITH PRIDE
MANY OF THEM DIED
THE WORLD MADE IT'S BREAD
FROM A PRAIRIE HOMESTEAD
SO MAY THEIR SOUL REST
FOR COMING OUT WEST

J. KEN MULLEN

JOHN FREEMAN MULLEN

CIRCA 1919

1896 - 1967

FLORENCE BELLE MULLEN

CIRCA 1919

1893 - 1980

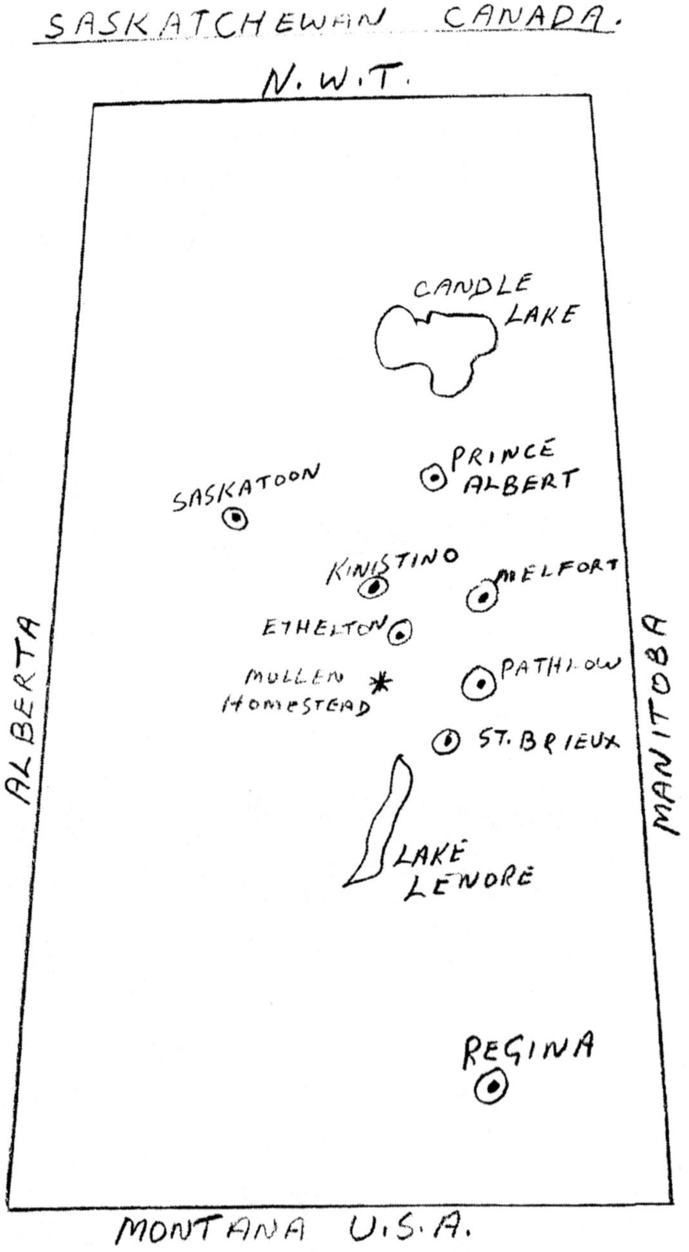

SASKATCHEWAN CANADA.

N.W.T.

CANDLE LAKE

PRINCE ALBERT

SASKATOON

KINISTINO

MELFORT

ETHELTON

MULLEN HOMESTEAD

PATHLOW

ST. BRIEUX

ALBERTA

MANITOBA

LAKE LENORE

REGINA

MONTANA U.S.A.

HOMESTEADER'S EQUIPMENT.

WOOD SWEDE SAW

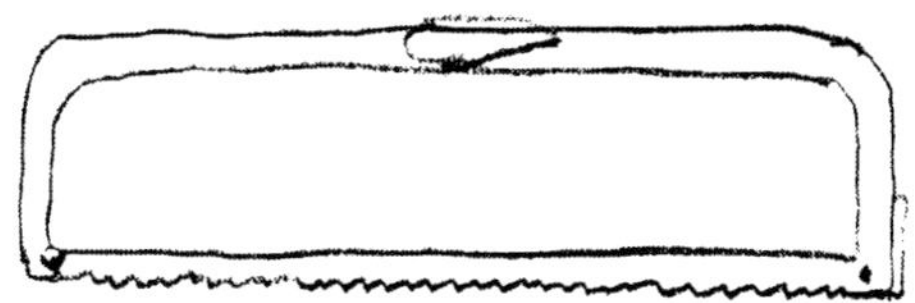

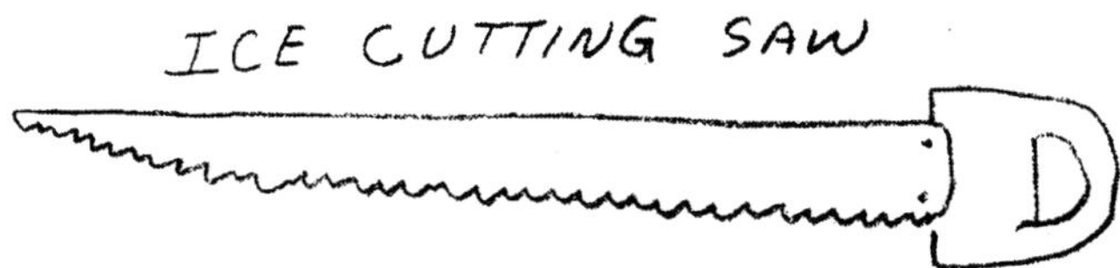

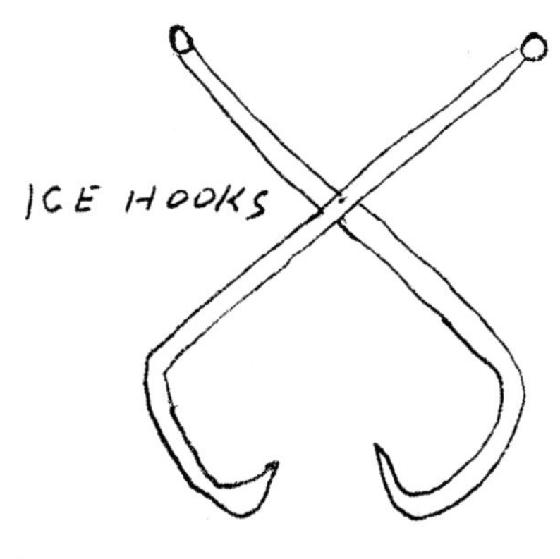

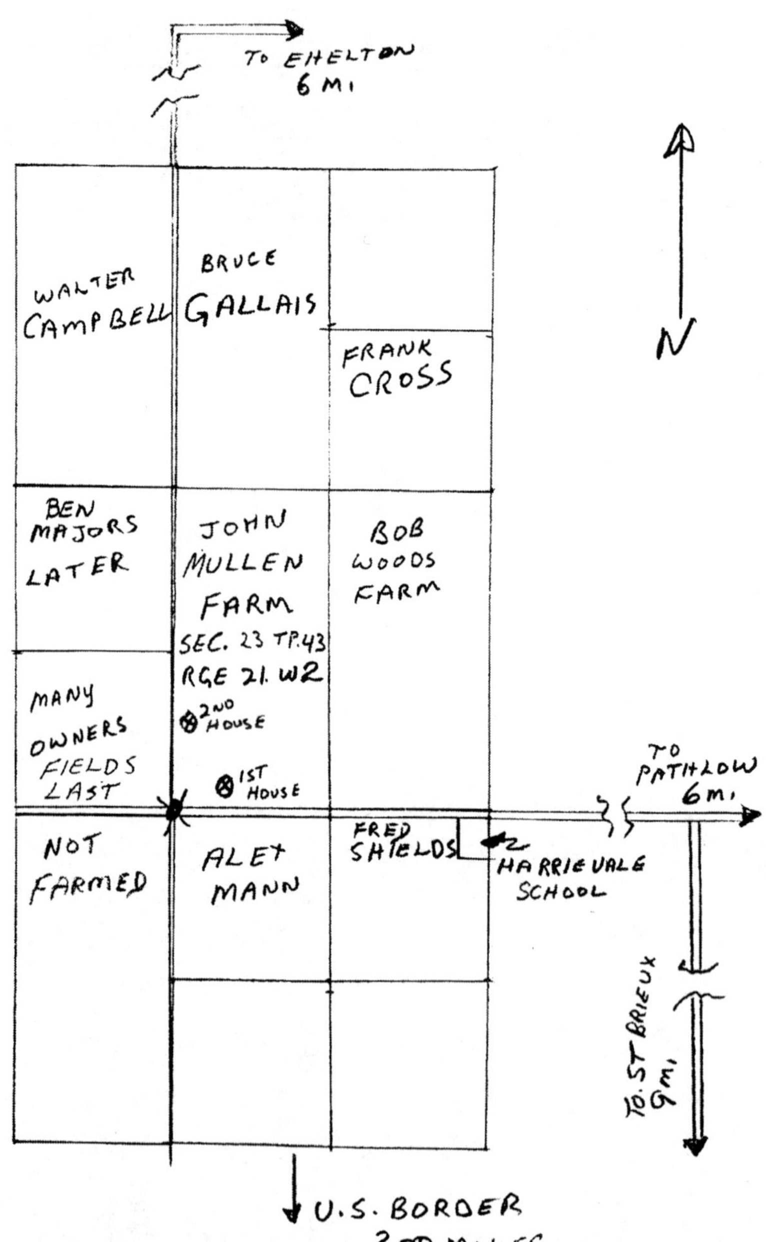
TO EHELTON
6 MI
N
WALTER
CAMPBELL
BRUCE
GALLAIS
FRANK
CROSS
BEN
MAJORS
LATER
JOHN
MULLEN
FARM
SEC. 23 TP.43
RGE 21. W2
2ND
HOUSE
1ST
HOUSE
BOB
WOODS
FARM
MANY
OWNERS
FIELDS
LAST
TO
PATHLOW
6 MI.
NOT
FARMED
ALEX
MANN
FRED
SHIELDS
HARRIEVALE
SCHOOL
TO ST BRIEUX
9MI.
U.S. BORDER
300 MILES

HEATER

TWO 45 GAL. DRUM
STACKED HEATER

GRAIN ELEVATOR

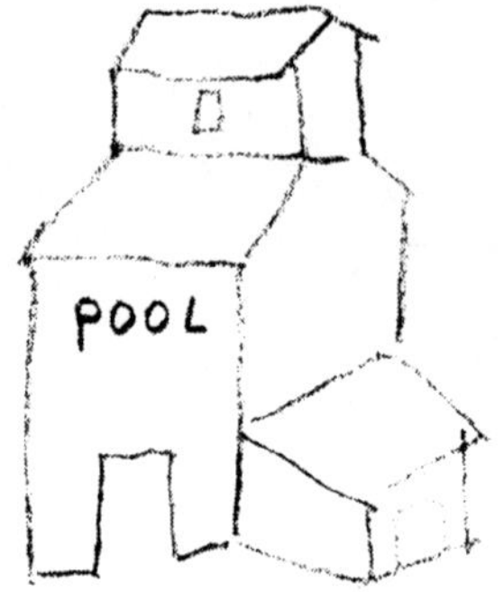

OUTHOUSE

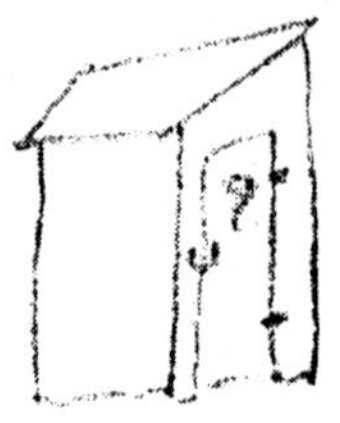

HAND WASHER

WELL PUMP

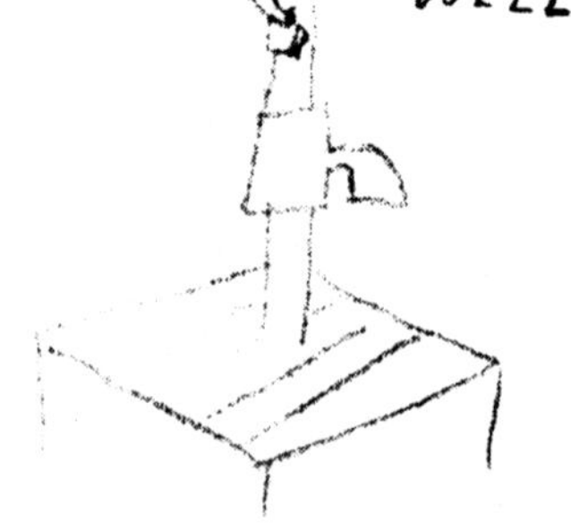

STOOK OF SHEAVES

SHEAVE OF GRAIN

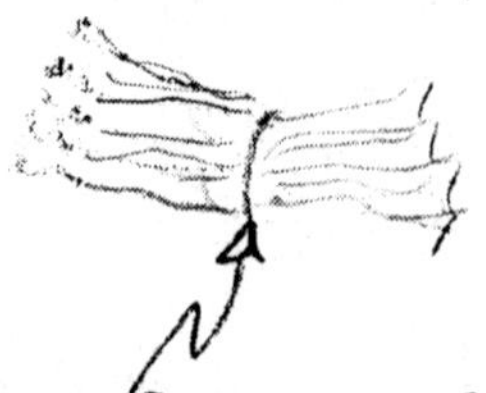

BINDER TWINE

SINGLE PLOW SHARE
1 OR 2 HORSES
DEPTH BY HEIGHT OF HANDLES

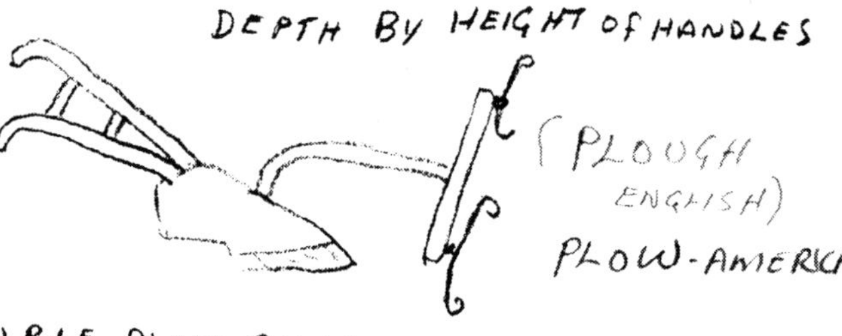

RIDING DOUBLE PLOW SHARE
4 HORSES
ADJUSTABLE DEPTH BY
LEVER

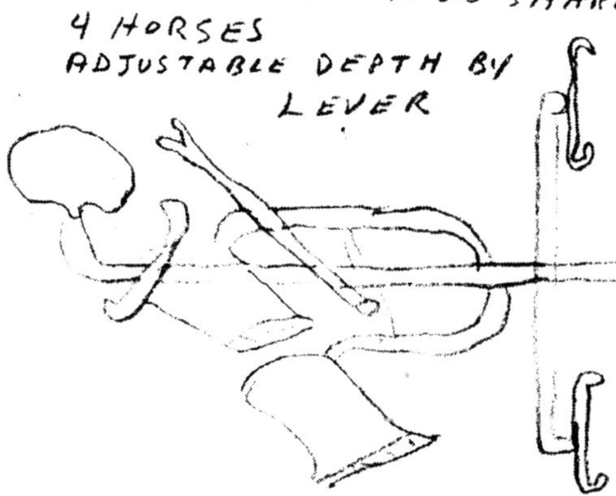

(PLOUGH
ENGLISH)
PLOW-AMERICAN

STONE BOAT

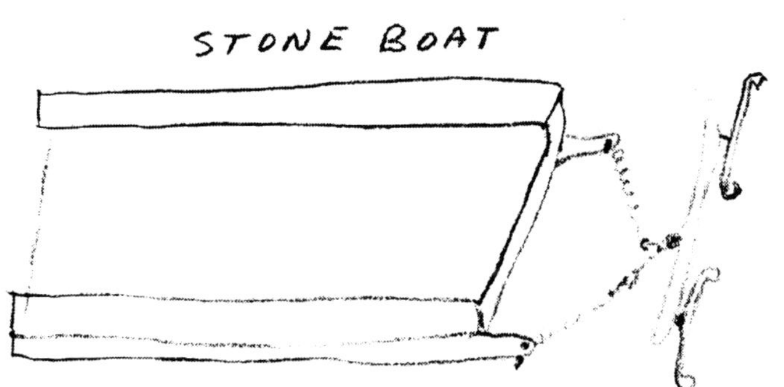

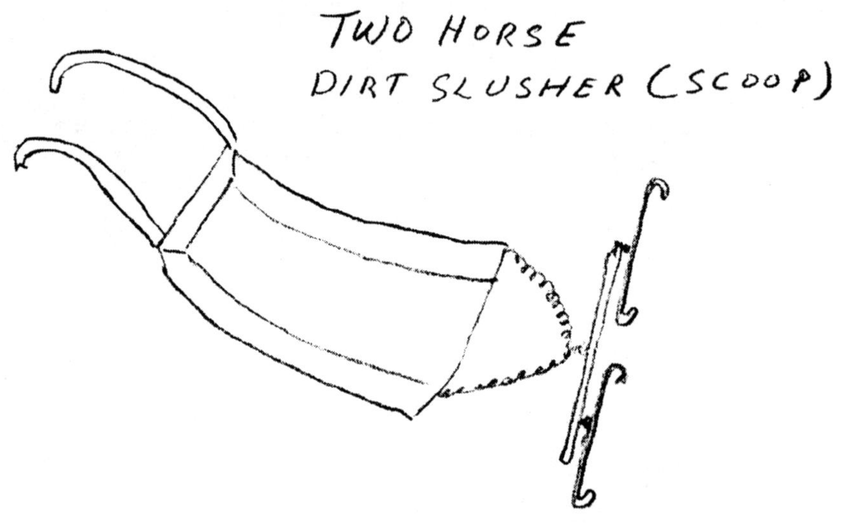

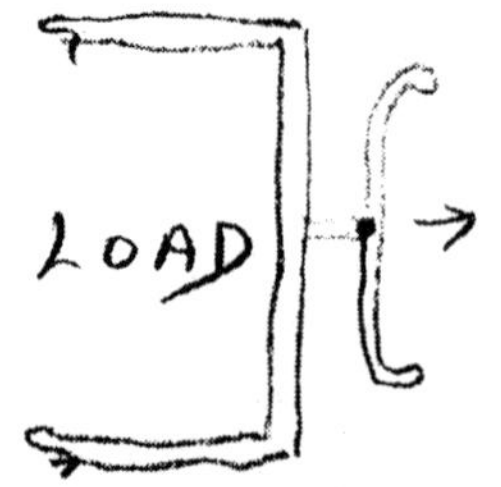

SINGLE TREE

TO ONE
HORSE HARNESS

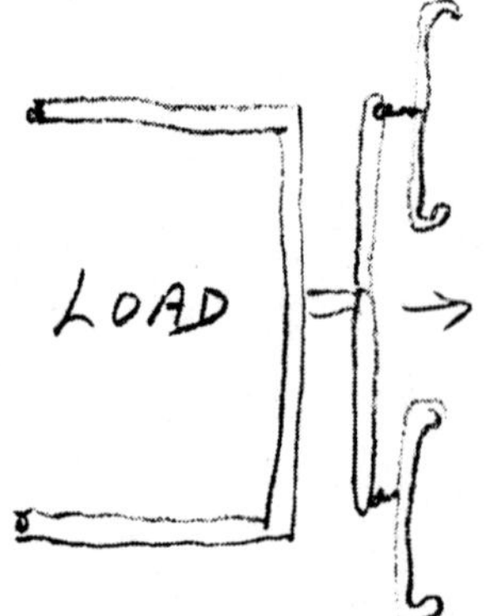

DOUBLE TREE

TO TWO HORSE
HARNESS

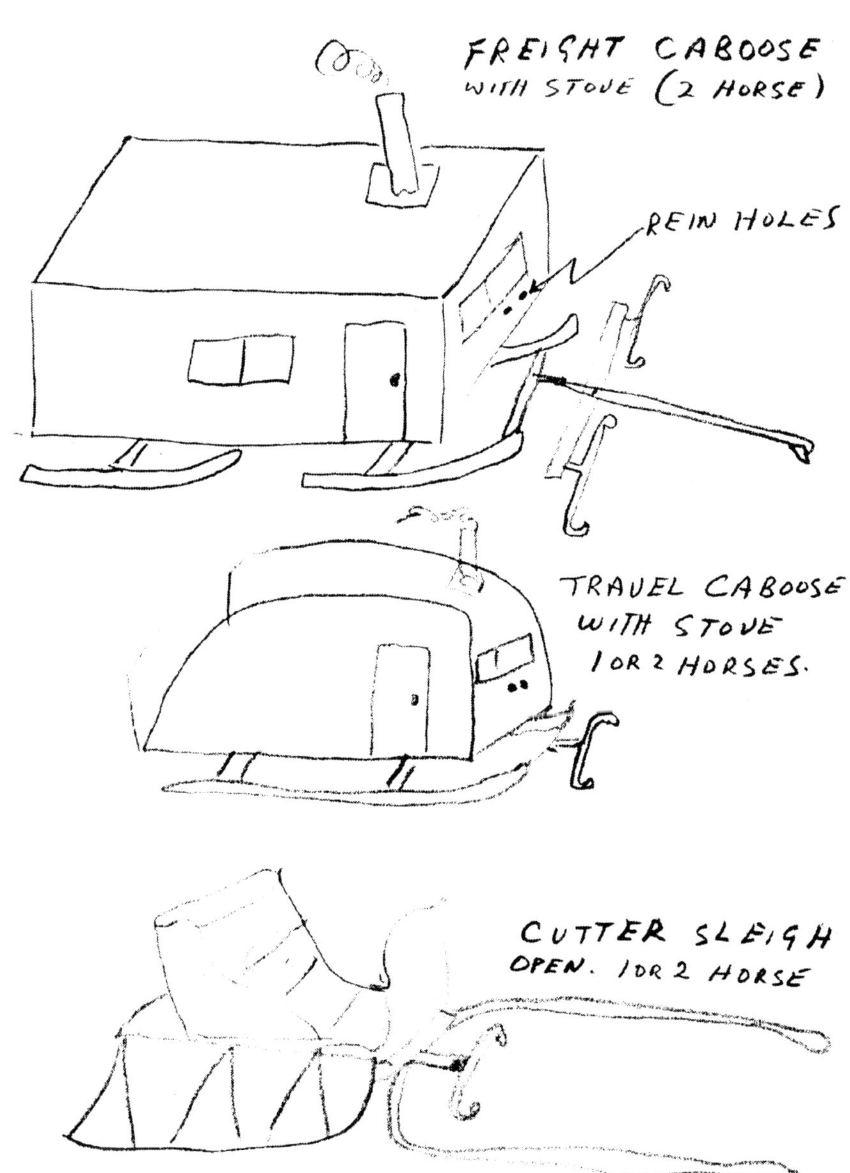
FREIGHT CABOOSE
WITH STOVE (2 HORSE)
REIN HOLES
TRAVEL CABOOSE
WITH STOVE
1 OR 2 HORSES.
CUTTER SLEIGH
OPEN. 1 OR 2 HORSE

Contents

CHAPTER 1

The Big Move

It was the 4th of February 1920. The train was heading across Saskatchewan toward the small town of Kinistino. It was a clear cold day, the click clack of the wheels on the frozen track were very loud in the 19 deg. below zero weather. The steam from the engine was freezing and dropping out as ice before it even reached the passenger cars at the rear. The bright glare on the white snow was nearly more than the eyes could stand.

John and his wife sat quietly with their thoughts. It had been a long trip from their home in Nova Scotia. This was a whole new world for both of them. John let the many reasons drift slowly through his mind. After the war the doctors recommended that John move to a dry climate because of the damage the gas had done to his lungs. You could get a half section of land through the Soldier Settlement Board with a long time to pay back He really didn't want to go back to painting after coming home. He and Florence had just got married and it would be a good time to make the move out west. Florence had a brother out in Saskatchewan and they could get land close to his farm and stay there until they were settled. There were so many things that said go west one would be stupid not to make the move. Now they were just a few miles away from their destination and all of a sudden it seemed too big to understand. Had they made the right move? Would they be able to make a living out here. Would the small war pension given them be enough to get started. Would Florence's brother meet them at the train? What was it like to farm where it was hot in the summer and very cold in the winter? How long would it take them to have a house of their own?

John's thoughts were interrupted by the conductor shouting. "Next stop Kinistino, all people stopping at Kinistino please get ready to leave the train".

John looked at Florence and said, "Well here we are I guess this is what we have been travelling for the last few days. Bundle up real good it is very cold out there."

Florence gave John a look that could have meant I'm not that stupid I can see that it is cold out there. But she did nothing for she had been having her own thoughts about coming out to this part of the world. This would be so much different than the job she had held in Boston during the war. Why neither one of them knew anything about farming let alone living in this harsh climate. She did not look upon this as the greatest thing in the world that was ever going to happen to them. It would be nice to see her brother again but all the rest of the family was back east and she was never that close to her brother and sister-in-law in the first place. That would have to be put by the wayside and try and make the best of the situation as it seemed this was to be their future.

The train finally came to a halt in front of the little station. The Conductor helped John and his wife from the train and they went into the waiting room. It was a small room attached to the Station Agents Office. There were benches all around the outside of the room and a potbelly stove in the centre. There was a roaring fire in the stove, the top had a red glow where the stove pipes left to cross the room to the chimney. The man standing behind the stove wearing the big coat and fur hat could only be one person.

"Hello Oscar," John said, "I could hardly recognize you in all those clothes, how have you been keeping?"

Oscar smiled and replied, "Hello John, hello Florence it has been a long time since we have seen each other. You won't be laughing at my dress after a few hours outside in this Saskatchewan weather. It is a lot colder here than back in Nova Scotia, you know".

Florence was the next one to speak, "Yes we have noticed that since we left Ontario. It has been really cold. What kind of a Godforsaken country is this anyway? Does it ever get warm here or does it snow all year?"

"Oh it can get warm" Oscar replied, "wait until summer comes and it gets to around 90 degrees and we have a real prairie thunder storm, then you will wish it winter and cold again. It isn't"t that bad you know, as long as you dress for it you will get along O.K. I agree it will not be as comfortable as what you were used to having in Boston and it is even a little rougher than what we had in Nova Scotia. But lets get heading for home it is about 18 miles and it will take us about 3 to 4 hours to make the trip. It is 11 o'clock now and I would like to get home by dark if possible. It gets dark just after 3 here and we cannot hurry the horses too much in this cold. We can talk on the way home, it will be warm in the caboose so you can come just as you are dressed".

The two big suit cases and old steamer trunk had been unloaded from the train and were now on the platform. The Station agent helped Oscar and John load them into the back of the caboose. The caboose was a big one, the top was made of canvas stretched over 2x2 and the bottom half was covered with shiplap and tar paper. There was a small stove in the centre with a pile of wood in a box near by. The chimney went through a piece of tin in the roof. There were seats around the front half. There was a small side door up front and a wide door in the back. The window in the front was in two pieces and could be opened by sliding one part past the other. The small holes under the window were used to slide the reins from the two horses so they could be steered from inside the caboose. This whole caboose was about six feet by ten feet and was all mounted on a double sleigh. This was a very good way to travel and also was warm in this cold weather. When travelling from town it was a way to keep the groceries from freezing let alone the passengers.

John went back into the station to get Florence while Oscar untied the team from the hitching post. They all got comfortable in the caboose for the long trip home. Oscar put a couple of sticks of wood on the fire and yelled "get-up" to the team and with a creaking of steel on the frozen snow the trip to Oscars house was under way.

Florence was the first to speak, "Oscar I am glad we are travelling in this little house, I had visions of a long trip in a open sleigh with frozen hands and feet. What do you call these things anyway"?

Oscar grinned and replied, "These are called a caboose, They sure have saved Stella and I from freezing to death more than once. It gives us a chance to go visit people in the winter time also we bring eggs to town to sell and they would freeze if it wasn't the caboose. You will see many different shapes and sizes of cabooses around the country, it just depends how you want to use them. Some people have only one seat a very small stove and pull them with only one horse. I like this big one because it will not tip over as easy in snow drifts and I can haul nearly everything I need. Anyway you will have lots of time to look over our different ways of travel in the next few years. You and John will have a lot of winters ahead of you yet if you are going to work at a homestead. How about telling me about the folks back home. It has been a long time since I have seen them, how is mom and dad? how are my two sisters doing? It gets lonely here we only go to town every week or so and even then there is sometimes no mail. If it wasn't for the Winnipeg Free Press and the Family Herald I don't know what we would do for news.

For the next couple of hours John, Florence and Oscar talked about Nova Scotia, Their families and friends, they all agreed it was going to be a different life for John and Florence but Oscar said, "They would soon be to busy to worry about how far they were from home. This was now their home and they might just as well make the best of what they had. It was going to be a long grind to make a half section of land into a farm. The land that they had applied for was completely covered with trees and they would have to be cleared before a crop could be sowed. He said the trees would come in handy to build their first house and for wood. Oscar then pointed out the window to their left. See that small town over there, that is called Ethelton. It is only six miles North of you farm. You will do a lot of your buying there. We are now about two thirds of the way home another hour should just about do it. We should get home just about dark. I hope Stella has got a good hot stew in this weather. We have a lot of stews with home made bread.

Oscar put some more wood on the fire, he let the team set their own pace. They also knew they were heading home and did not even need to be steered. They also knew a good warm barn and straw with oats was waiting for them.

The next hour passed quickly and the next thing they knew the team was turning into the driveway of Oscar's farm. The team stopped in front of the house. Oscar said he would put the team away if John would unload the caboose, he told Florence to go inside and see Stella.

The house was made of squared logs with small round trees split into quarters and jammed between the logs. These chinks as they were called were covered with mud. This made a nice warm home in the winter and was quite cool in the summer. The main part of the house was only one story high. The back part was two stories high, this was where the bedrooms were. The living room kitchen was a good size with a big kitchen stove at one end and a big sheet iron heater at the other end by the bottom of the stairs. The heat would rise up the stairway and keep the bedrooms warm. The first thing Florence saw as she entered the room was Stella standing over the stove stirring a pot of stew. The smell was one of the most welcome things that Florence could remember.

Stella looked up and grinned at Florence. She waved one hand toward the front room and said, "Take your coat off and sit down, my goodness it sure is good to see someone from home. We will probably be up all night talking. I bet you are tired from your trip. It must feel good to sit down and not be moving for a change".

Florence hung her coat on the pegs by the door and went on into the living-room part. "Yes" she said, "It will be good to sit still for a while. You have a comfortable looking place here Stella, it is good of you to put us up until we get a place of our own to live. Can I help you in any way?".

"No", Stella answered her, "eveything is ready for supper. You and I will just sit and talk while John moves the stuff into the house and Oscar looks after the team".

The two women sat and talked for a hour then Stella put supper on the table. It was just a plain farm type supper but everyone ate until they could hardly move. This cold weather and the smell from the kitchen had made everyone very hungry.

After supper the women cleaned up the kitchen. Oscar went out to do the chores in the barn. John wanted to help but Oscar said he would have a chance to help tomorrow when he had working clothes on instead of his Sunday go to church Meeting clothes. A couple more hours of talking was spent around the front room stove. Then after a cup of coffee and some jam sandwiches John and Florence went to their bedroom upstairs and Oscar and Stella went to their bedroom down stairs. They had cautioned John and Florence to leave the door open in their bedroom or it would get as cold as outside.

John set down the coal oil lamp and said to Florence. "I guess we had better get to sleep if I am to start tomorrow at learning how to be a farmer".

Florence laughed at this and replied, "I don't think you will do much farming in this kind of weather. I would think that just keeping the fire going would be a full time job".

John said, "I have a lot to learn about keeping stock and those kind of things other than what I learned about horses in the Army I know very little about animals. Anyway are you sorry we have made the big move?".

Florence answered with. "Ask me that question a few years from now when we have been farming for a while. Until then I will reserve my judgement".

With that they went to sleep and the only noise that could be heard was the fire crackling down stairs and the sharp cracks of the frost in the roof of the house. It had been a long tiring day this first day of becoming a homesteader.

CHAPTER 2

The Homestead Logger

The next morning about 6:30 John heard Oscar stoking up the big stove down stairs. Then he heard him lighting a fire in the cook stove. The room felt cold but not unbearable. John got out of bed and started to light the lamp. Florence poked her head out from under the covers and said. "What are you doing poking around in the dark?"

John lit the lamp and said. "Oscar is up and I think I well get up and see what goes on around a farm this early in the morning. There is no reason for you to get up yet, the fire has just been lit and it will take a while before breakfast can be started".

John got his work clothes out of the trunk and the heavy felt boots that had been recommended that he have if he was going to live out in that cold place called Saskatchewan. He got dressed, picked up his heavy jacket, rubbers and the fur cap with ear protectors. When he arrived at the bottom of the stairs Oscar turned around from the cook stove and said.

"What are you doing up so early you should stay in bed until the house gets a little warmer".

John looked at Oscar and replied, "Well if I am going to be a farmer then I might as well learn to do things right. But why do you get up in the middle of the night in the winter time? I could see it if it was daylight out."

Oscar shook his head and replied, "Today we have to go and cut wood for the fire and lumber. We have to go out and feed the horses and cows, we will milk the cows and then separate the milk and then have breakfast. By that time it will be time to feed the pigs and chickens. Then we will have to water the cows and horses and then it will be daylight and time to hook up to the sleigh and go cutting wood."

The men put on their rubbers over the felt boots, heavy jackets and fur hats. Oscar put on his mitts and asked John. "Where are your mitts? It is 30 degrees below zero out there right now. If you touch any of the steel door locks outside your hands will stick to them as if they were glued."

John looked at Oscar and said. "I only have gloves. I never thought about mitts."

"Well here is a extra pair.", Oscar offered. "those gloves will be alright in the warmer weather but mitts are better in the cold because your fingers will keep each other warm."

The men stepped out through the double door and headed out to the barn. It was only about 200 feet to the barn, the snow squeaked beneath your feet and your cheeks tingled with the frosty air. The barn was warm inside and Oscar remarked.

"This is the warmest toilet on the whole place. That one I put in the basement is not bad but still cold. That one out side would breeze your behind off even if it had a fur seat."

Both men laughed at this remark. Then Oscar began to show John how to do the morning chores. First he put some oat straw in the mangers for the four horses and two cows. Then he put a small amount of oats in the manger boxes. Next the manure from behind the horses and cows was thrown out the back door on top of a already high pile. Oscar explained it would be hauled away in the spring and put on the field as fertilizer. Next Oscar took the pail he had brought from the house, sat on a small stool and milked the two cows. Then the two men went back to the house with the milk. Oscar set the pail of milk on the kitchen counter for Stella to separate the cream. Both men then washed their hands and faces in a small wash basin, they had got the warm water from the reservoir at the back of the stove. The dirty water was thrown into a bucket which would be thrown outside later, also more snow would be brought inside and put in the reservoir to melt and make more soft water.

Breakfast was ready so the four of them sat down and began to eat. First was a bowl of cracked wheat porridge, made from Oscar's own crop. Then two fried eggs, fried potatoes, salt cured pork an couple pieces of toast and a couple cups of coffee. Oscar had said at the beginning of the meal that one had to eat lots because there would be no more until dinner at noon.

While the men were finishing their breakfast Stella took some of the fresh milk from the pail and put in in a container for use at meal time. The rest she put through the cream separator. She put the cream into one container and the skim milk was put back into the pail to be mixed with grain to feed to the pigs.

Oscar turned to Stella and said. "Make up a couple of lunches because John and I are going to cut wood today. It will warm up quite a bit yet and there is no wind so it should be a good day for bush work."

Stella nodded and said. "You are sure putting John to work right away aren't you? My heavens they just got here yesterday. What is the big hurry?"

"Well" Oscar replied. "John wants to be a farmer and he will never learn any younger so we may as well get started. Anyway he will get a share of the lumber from the bigger logs and the fire wood will help keep him and Florence warm."

Oscar and John went back out to the barn. Oscar mixed the

skin milk with some barley added the vegetable peels he had brought from the house and went out behind the barn. as he started to dump the feed into a trough five pigs came running out from under a straw pile. Oscar turned to John and said. "You sure don't throw any junk away with thess. animals around, they will eat anything that is left over."

Then Oscar went to a small shed beside the barn took out a pail of grain and went over to the chicken house. He opened the door and spread the grain into the feeders for the chickens. Oscar told John, "Stella would look after the chickens the rest of the day. What little money they got from the few eggs they sold was hers."

They went back to the barn and Oscar handed the pail to John and said. "You go up to the house and get some warm water to thaw out the pump and I will harness up the team." When John got back Oscar had let the other two horses and the two cows out the back into the corral they were standing by the well waiting for their morning drink. Oscar told John to pour the water down the pump and to pump water into the big galvanized trough that was already half full of ice. The horses and cows drank their fill and Oscar was now leading the team out for their morning drink. After they had finished drinking he hooked them up to a sleigh with just a bottom and bunks for hauling logs. They drove up by the house after they had put some straw on the back of the sleigh. Oscar went into the house to get their lunch. When he came out he was carrying two ten pound pails with covers on and one pail with a couple of cups inside and package of tea. He put these on the sleigh yelled get up to the team and away they went to cut wood.

They travelled about a mile along the road then turned up a small road into the bush. They stopped at a small clearing, there was already a fair size pile of good sized logs at one side of the clearing.

Oscar explained to John, "The big logs we will take to the saw mill before spring and get them cut into lumber. Old Mike that runs the mill will keep a third of the lumber and we can bring home the rest. You can take some John as you will need it when you start your own place. We will snake out the bigger logs to this pile and the smaller ones we will take back to the farm for fire wood Let's leave the sleigh here and tie old Tom to a tree with some straw. We will take the mare Bess with us into the woods and you can use her to snake logs out to the clearing. Bring along the log chain and single tree. I will bring the lunches and some straw to start a fire.

Oscar led the way along a winding trail back into the bush. On the way in he explained to John that no one cared about cutting the trees because the land had to be cleared someday anyway.

It had not snowed since the last time Oscar had been in here cutting wood so the trail was easy to follow. The snow was not that deep which surprised John he thought it would be much deeper than it was. But Oscar explained that the snow does not ever really get that deep it just does not go away until spring.

Oscar took his axe and cut some branches off a couple of dead trees put some straw under them and in no time had a good fire going. He put some good size logs on the fire then filled the empty tin with snow and sat it by the fire. He then sat the other two cans with the lunch in them on a stump close to the fire then said to John.

"This will keep our lunch from freezing, and we can have tea to drink all day. If we let them freeze you won't be able to chew the damn sandwiches and you will be surprised how thirsty you get working out in the dry snow.

After Oscar had finished this he showed John how to hook up the single tree with the log chain, hook it on to the end of a log that had been cut, get on to the back of the horse and take them out to the clearing. He told John to put the big ones with the pile to go to the mill, the smaller ones by the sleigh to go home and the Birch logs in a separate pile because they were good hard wood for all most anything around the farm from sleigh runners to plow handles.

John soon learned the difference between the white and black Poplar trees. He also learned the hard way that if you took the corners to close you had one Hell of a job to get the log you were pulling unhooked from the stumps that seemed to be all over the place.

Every few trips John would stop for a cup of tea and get warm by the fire. If he got ahead of Oscar he would help limb and top the trees. He soon found out that you sure had to keep the axe sharp to cut the frozen trees.

At noon the men stopped for lunch. They fed the horses the straw that was left then sat beside the fire to have their sandwiches and drink some more hot tea. After lunch they continued to cut and snake out logs until about 2:30. Oscar said they should load the sleigh and head for home before it got dark and colder. As they were picking up their equipment Oscar turned to John and said. "You can keep track of the number of cups of tea you have drank by how many yellow holes there are in the snow." Both men laughed and continued out to the sleigh. They loaded the smaller logs, hooked up the team and headed for home.

It was dark when John and Oscar arrived at the farm. They unhooked the team and left the sleigh beside the wood pile. Oscar said they would unload it to-morrow. He told John that they would have a week of wood sawing bee's soon and that he would enjoy them.

After the men had watered the stock again and put them all in the barn Oscar explained to John that they should be fed hay at night. He said that he didn't have much hay but if he only used it once a day it may last until spring.

After supper the men went to milk the cows and finish up the chore. When they returned to the house they sat around and talked with the women. Everyone had put in a good days work so they went to bed early. As John was blowing out the lamp to crawl into bed he said to Florence, "I don't know if I learned anything about farming today but I guess I am now a first class Homestead Logger."

CHAPTER 3

The Ice Haul

One morning at the breakfast table Oscar announced to John that they were going to go cutting ice today. John sat there with a puzzled look on his face then he asked Oscar.

"Why in the Hell would you go cutting ice in a county like this when it was all around?"

Oscar laughed, thumped the table with his hand and replied. "It won't be all around us this summer. Some good home made ice cream will go pretty good when she is about 80 or 90 degrees in the shade."

John did not say any more about the ice but finished his breakfast then went out to help finish the chores. He could do all the chores now and enjoyed being able to look after the animals. He hooked up the team to the sleigh like Oscar had asked. The sleigh had a box on it now. It was the same type of box that was used to haul grain and many other things. John had driven the team over by the tool shed where Oscar waited with the tools for cutting ice. This was going to prove to be another different day on the homestead.

The men travelled about three miles, partly by road and partly across open swamp land that Oscar said was not a bad place to get hay in the summer time. They drove out onto a small lake with the team and sleigh. When they got to a opening in the ice Oscar stopped the team an said to John.

"We are lucky someone has been cutting ice here yesterday and the hole is not frozen over thick. This will save us a lot of work not having to cut the hole ourselves."

Oscar then proceeded to show John how to cut ice. With the big long saw the ice was cut into good size blocks then broken away from the main ice with a axe. A big set of tongs were snapped onto the blocks. A chain was hooked onto the tongs then fastened to the back of the sleigh. The team was made to go ahead and the block of ice was pulled out of the water. The team would then be backed up to the block and it was loaded onto the sleigh. This was repeated over and over again until the sleigh box was full of ice. Now the men put the tools on top of the load and headed back to the farm.

On the way back home John told Oscar about some of his experiences overseas during the war. He was always willing to talk about the war if people would listen. The war was still real to him and many a night he still woke up in a cold sweat from bad dreams. He had been in all the major battles and none of them had been very nice. He had not only lost many buddies but also two brothers during the war. He was still anti German and would join up tomorrow to fight for his country. A lot of people out on the farms did not understand this and sometimes showed their lack of interest in this war talk. This used to make John mad but he never let on. He just put it down to the fact that the people here had been so far away from the war that they just did not understand what really had gone on over there.

When the men arrived back at the house they put the team in the barn and fed them. They went to the house for dinner. Out here the meals were a little different than back east. It was Breakfast in the morning. Dinner at noon Supper at night and Lunch before you went to bed at night. One thing was for sure people knew how to eat out here on the homestead. When you work hard all day it was only right that you had good meals. The main parts of the meals were made up of potatoes and meat. It was not unusual to have potatoes at all three meals. Fried in the morning. Boiled at noon and baked or mashed with gravy at night. There was also turnip, parsnip, carrots, beets to be had with the meal. These were kept in the basement or root cellar below the house. They were covered with dry sand to keep them fresh but also to keep them from freezing. The cold weather was the worst enemy to the farmer. He could grow almost all his food as long as he could keep it to use in the long winter months.

After dinner John and Oscar went out to the barn and hooked up the team to the sleigh and headed up behind the house into the trees. There was a hole in the ground about ten feet deep. Oscar backed the sleigh up to the hole and the men started to unload the blocks of ice into the hole. They had to break the ice apart because by this time they had frozen together. When they had finished Oscar explained to John why they were putting ice down the hole.

"When we have filled the hole with ice John," Oscar said, "we will leave it until after we have cut up our wood pile over there. Then we will pick up all the sawdust that was mixed with snow and cover up the ice. When we get the logs that we have cut into lumber we will build a shed over the top of the ice. Some people just cover the hole with straw, but I think it is better to put a shed over the top with maybe a little straw over the sawdust. Anyway it makes a good place to store meat for a short length of time. Under these trees it will stay quite cool in here. On July the 1st we will treat you and Florence to some home made ice cream in the summer time.

"That sounds good," John replied, "That's one promise we will make you keep. I hope we are in a house of our own before then. Maybe we will have to rent a place or something. We can't be staying with you and Stella for ever."

"Well we will worry about that after the spring breakup." Oscar said,,"Maybe we can find a place close to your homestead for you to stay, I hear the old Joe Bell's house is empty. If you could stay there it would give you a chance to put in a garden do some work on your own place.

By now the two men had got themselves into a good routine about doing the chores. Some days they even had some time to spare, which was rare on a homestead. The main thing was John had been in on a ice haul and now knew the in's and out's about putting up ice for the summer.

CHAPTER 4

A Lumber Haul and Wood Bee

After days of cutting logs and hauling ice it was about time to haul the logs to have them cut into lumber before the spring break up. With this in mind John and Oscar hooked up both teams of horses each to a sleigh with bunks. Oscar had borrowed the second sleigh from his neighbour. This would happen quite often between the homesteaders as it was too costly to have too much equipment.

The men had headed down to where they had skidded the logs to earlier. They loaded each sleigh in order. The bigger logs had to be rolled up poles laid against the sleigh to get them loaded. This was hard work and it was easy to work up a sweat when you had on a lot of clothes. Oscar suggested that they take off their jackets while they were working so that they would have them to put on when they finished loading.

When the men had both sleighs loaded they drove back to the farm and put the horses in the barn for feeding and went and had dinner themselves. The days were getting longer now so they would be able to take their loads of logs to Ethelton after dinner. It was only about 5 miles from Oscar's farm to town. Mike Demeter had a small sawmill behind his blacksmith shop. He had made the thing himself in his spare time. It was not what you would call a real sawmill but it would cut up logs into rough lumber and 2x4. This was plenty good enough for making buildings around the farm. The price also was right for Mike would keep one third of the lumber for doing the cutting. He would also keep the slabs from the outside of the logs and use them for his own fire wood.

The men made the trip to town after dinner in good time. The roads were good and were free of snow drifts. They unloaded the logs behind the small mill and talked to Mike to make arrangements to have the logs cut up into lumber. It was decided that they had about fourteen loads to haul and this would take them until next Monday or Tuesday if the weather held. It would take them a couple of days to cut the lumber and about another two days to haul it home. It looked like the next couple of weeks would be busy.

After the arrangements were made the men went to the store and picked up a few things. Then they went to the Post Office to pick up the mail. It was always nice to get the mail and see what was going on in the rest of the world. Sometimes you would get a letter from back home and this would make you feel a bit homesick for old Nova Scotia. John liked very much going to the Post Office as the man who ran it had also been overseas in the war. George also liked to talk to John about their experiences. Sometimes Oscar would have to break up the conversations or they would never get home before dark or even later.

The trip home went fast as the sleighs were empty and the horses would trot a good distance of the way. The men got home in good time and the women were glad to receive the mail and small items from the store. That night everyone was quiet as they sat around the table and read the papers that had been picked up in town.

The men hauled logs everyday except Sunday till the following Monday night. They had taken fourteen loads all-together to Mike's sawmill. The next day they would start cutting it up into lumber.

The next morning the men were up real early so they could be at Mikes place just after daylight to get started. They took their lunch with them because they did not want to put Mikes wife out and also they did not want to take too much time for dinner. When they arrived in town they put the sleighs by the little mill and took the horses over to the community barn. They had brought along feed for the horses so they stored that in the corner to be used at noon. By the time they got back across the street to Mikes place he had the gas engine running and was turning over the saws to get ready to receive the logs.

Oscar and John would roll the logs onto a row of rollers and then push them into the big saw. Mike would work the few controls at the other end . Once the slabs were cut off the sides of the log Mike would then set the saw to cut either boards or two by fours. It was not the most accurate way of cutting rough lumber but it worked. Anyway the horses and chickens didn't care if the barns and coops had all the same thickness of lumber. Another thing Mike might be a little hard to understand when he talked in his broken English but he sure as Hell knew how to handle and make machinery work for him.

The three of them worked like this until noon. Oscar and John went and fed the horses. When they came back Mike insisted that they eat with them. But both Oscar and John said they didn't want to get out of their heavy clothes so they would eat in the Blacksmith shop. Mike said, "O.K. but his wife would send them out a pot of tea. They agreed to this arrangement. It was quite warm sitting on the workbench by the window. The sun was coming through the glass and made the meal pleasant.

The men worked until about the middle of the afternoon then shut down the mill. Oscar and John loaded the lumber on the sleighs and headed for home. Mike had said he would look after the rest of the lumber and slabs that had to be moved.

The next day was handled in just about the same way. They had completed cutting all the logs and would have to haul lumber for another two days. When they had all the lumber home Oscar told John that some belonged to him, and he could take it when he needed. John had said thanks but it was also good to learn what to do with the logs when they were cut.

Oscar looked at John and laughed the said, 'You may now know how to cut and haul lumber but next week we will learn you how to cut fire wood. It has all been set up to have a wood cutting bee startling Monday. You will enjoy that but you will be tired at night after a full day of cutting wood.

John said,"That he was looking forward to working at a wood cutting bee".

On Monday morning Oscar was up early. He and John were on the way over to the Joe Cosman place to cut wood. They just had the team and sleigh because it was only about a mile and half away. When they got there some of the other people had arrived. In total there were seven men all together. The idea was that for the next six days the men would cut wood at each other place for one day. One of the men owned the saw and he would be paid one dollar a day for whom the wood was being cut. John was the extra man but it was always helpful to have as many as possible. They would even cut wood for one day at the owner of the saws place. A homestead used a lot of wood during the year. There was not only the cold winters to heat the house but all the cooking was done on a wood stove. With the canning and so on in summer a lot of trees were used up as fuel.

John was quite interested in the way the wood cutting was done. The saw blade was on a small sleigh with a motor. The saw was driven by a belt from the motor to a mandrel with the blade on the end. Beside the saw blade a steel bar stuck out from each side. All the men but one would lift the log that was to be cut up on to the steel bars.

They would push the log along the steel bars until it was the right length for fire wood. Then they would all push the log into the saw with their hips. The other man would be on the other side of the saw. He would grab the cut piece of wood and throw it over his shoulder. By the time the log was cut up the men would be ready with another log. When the man who was throwing the cut wood got tired he moved to the end of the line and in this way they could cut wood all day. When they had finished at the end of the day there would be a pile of wood about fifty feet long and eight feet high. This would be a good help in the next year's wood supply.

There was always something to remember about these wood cutting bee's. If nothing else the women tried to out do each other with their meals that they gave the men at noon. It was a wonder that the men were able to work after the size of some of the dinners they put away.

On Saturday night John was telling Florence about the weeks work and how tired he was after six days of wood cutting. He told her that there was one thing he would never forget. This is the way he told the story to her.

"We were going back to cut wood after dinner one day." he said,"and one of the men noticed a Partridge on a limb of a tree about a hundred yards away. He said hey John why don't you shoot that bird for us you must be a good shot weren't you in the Army?"

His answer to the man was, "I was in the Artillery and shot nothing but big Howitzer guns which is a little different from a rifle.". Well the banter kept up until Walter came out of the barn with his rifle and said "Here John show us what a good shot you are, pick off that Partridge for us". Well I fooled around with the gun adjusting the sights, looking down the barrel at the bird just hoping to hell that bird would fly away. But as luck would have it the bird just sat there and looked at us. I had to take a chance so I took a deep breath and pulled the trigger. Do you know that damn bird fell right out of the tree. I had shot it's head right off. Nobody said a word so I told them if they wanted any good shooting done just to call. I sure hope they don't John laughed. At cutting lumber and wood I may be O.K. but as a marksman I have a long ways to go.

CHAPTER 5

Spring Breakup and House Hunting

The weather was now starting to warm up and the days getting a lot longer. In some places the ground was starting to show through the snow. The sun had some real heat in the day time even though it still froze at night. It looked like spring was finally getting close by. Everyone was pleased with the coming of the warm weather and the joys of spring after a long hard cold Saskatchewan winter.

John and Florence were especially glad to see spring on its way. They were more than thankful to have had a place to stay for the rest of the winter, but would be glad to get into a place of their own. Florence had told John more than once that she could not stand much more of two women in the same kitchen. She was not being in any way unthankful for the help they had been getting it was just that in the middle of winter you didn't ever have a chance to be by yourself or take a walk outside. But today they were both looking forward to the trip they were going to take over to the house about two miles from Oscar's farm. They had been told that they could stay there for the summer if they wanted. They had hooked up one of Oscar's teams to the small sleigh and were going over to look the place over. It didn't take them long to get there and they were soon taking a peek at the place that might be their first home.

The door of the house was not locked so they just walked inside. There was no reason to lock up a place here as no one would bother the place even if they did go by. And it was very seldom that anyone would be going by other than people that lived around here. They did not say much as they looked through the small house. It had a fair sized kitchen and two small bedrooms. There was a trap door that went down into a small cellar. The roof looked alright but you could see out through the cracks in some of the wall boards. John was the first one to speak.

"Well Flossie" he said, "If I put some tar paper on the walls it won't be too bad of a place."

Florence gave John a dirty look. She did not really liked to be called Flossie but Oscar and John had been doing this lately but she wouldn't let on she didn't like being called that name. Finally she said.

"It sure isn't a mansion but it will be nice to be into a place of our own."

They went outside to size up the situation there. John looked at the outhouse with the door hanging on one hinge and said.

"I will sure have to get that door fixed or you will never move into this place with it like that.

"You can bet your boots I won't" was Florence's reply, "We will have to do a lot of work before we move in here. It looks like there might have been a garden over in that area?".

"Yes", John answered, "It looks that way. It also looks like that was a well so I guess there is water close by".

They walked out to the barn and looked it over. It seemed to be usable and plenty big enough for what they would need. They would only have a couple of horses and a cow or two to start with. They would have to raise a few chickens also to keep them in eggs. They walked around a bit more then went back to the sleigh.

John said to Florence, "I guess I will have to go to town and buy the supplies we need to fix up the house. If we wait too long the snow will be gone and the roads will be a mess of mud for a while".

"Yes", Florence replied, "I will have to get a order into Eatons for all the kitchen equipment that we need and work clothes and all that kind of stuff".

On the way back they talked about all the things they would have to do in the next little while before spring breakup.

That night John asked Oscar for the Eaton's Catalogue. And Oscar replied. "Don't you get enough of reading that thing up in the outhouse or are you really going to buy something?".

With this remark everyone laughed but some how Stella still gave Oscar a look that told him his jokes weren't funny.

Florence made out a order for just about everything that was to be used in the house, from dishes to bed blankets. John also ordered a lot of work clothes and boots, he even ordered harness for the team that he was going to have to buy. When they had finished the order they looked it over and Florence said.

"We will need a wagon train to move all this stuff from the train station to the house."

John replied with, "Thank God for my war pension cheque."

The next day John took the team and went to Meskanaw to get the building supplies needed to fix up the house. This town was only about ten miles from Oscar's farm. It was due west of Ethelton about six miles. It had an lumber yard and there was none at Ethelton. John mailed the order to Eatons, picked up a few things at the store and headed home. The roads were starting to break up fast now and he would be lucky if he would get his supplies delivered today while the roads were passable.

John made the round trip with no trouble, but it was lucky for the next day was really warm and the snow just seemed to disappear before one's eyes. The roads now were a mud hole in the day time and a frozen mess of ice and ruts at night. It was impossible to travel by day with the sleigh and the use of a wagon was next to impossible. The wagon would either sink in the mud or bounce the life out of you when the ground was frozen.

Some days it would snow a little and some days it would rain. In between it would be warm and sunny. It was for sure that the spring breakup was here. With the road next to impossible to use Oscar said it was a good time to spread the manure that had been piled out behind the barn. He explained to John how this would be done.

We will use a stone boat to haul the manure he said, this is a low shallow box about six feet by eight feet and one foot deep. The box is mounted on to log runners that are cut at the front at about forty-five degrees. This whole piece of equipment is pulled by a team of horses. The reason it is called a stone boat is it is used to remove stones from the fields, it is easier to roll the stones on to the low box than to lift them up into a wagon. There are a lot of stones in this part of the country so the stone boat comes in handy. It also is handy for spreading manure on the fields when the ground is half bare of snow.

For the next few days the men hauled manure from the barn area and from the chicken house area. This would be good fertilizer and was spread fairly heavy in the garden area.

John and Florence had by now witnessed their first spring break up and were both surprised at how nice it was getting to be with some of the trees starting to come into bud. They would soon be moving into their own house, they would have to get busy working on the place so they could move in soon.

CHAPTER 6

Spring and a Place to Live

For a few days now John and Florence had been walking over to their house to work. Sometimes they would cut across country and make the distance ever shorter. They would take their lunch with them as now the weather was warm enough for them to get along without a fire. They had put the tar paper on the outside of the walls and made a counter in the kitchen. John had repaired the outhouse and would dig a new hole when the frost was out of the ground. They enjoyed this working together on the house. It gave them a chance to make plans for the coming year. They had so many thing to do it seemed there would not be enough time to get everything done in time. At dinner time they started to make plans for the most important jobs they would have to take care of in the next week or so.

John and Florence sat down on the front steps with their lunch. John started with. "I guess the first thing we should get is a team of horses and a wagon so we can haul the things we need and work the garden for spring planting.

Florence nodded her head in agreement and replied. "The horses will be expensive this time of the year. Stella told me no one likes to part with them in the spring, they are easy to keep care of in the summer as they can be put out to pasture as long as there is water around.

They are no trouble at all."

"Yes I know", John sighed. "But there is not much we can do about that. It would not be to easy to get along without them and Oscar said maybe I could get some work on the roads if I have my own team. That would give us a chance to pick up a little extra money. With all the stuff we ordered and the rest that we need that should just about clean us out of our last dollar."

Florence waited a couple of minutes before she replied. "At least we will have a start on our own. Lets get to town and buy the things we need to get moved over here".

They both agreed to this, so they finished their dinner and went back to work.

The next day John did not go over to the house to work. Instead he borrowed a bridle and halter from Oscar and set out to walk over to the Taylor farm north of Ethelton. It was about ten or eleven miles but he did not intend to walk both ways. He intended to buy a couple of horses from Mr. Taylor. Oscar had said they raised more horses than they used on the farm and made extra money selling them to the other farmers. He told John that the horses would not be cheap but they would be in good shape and there would be a good selection to pick from. John knew some about horses from his experience in the army and he had learned a lot more since coming out west. He thought he would like to get a couple of good sized horses because they would be needed to do all the work around the farm. It was a nice day for walking and he arrived at the Taylor farm just before dinner time. When Mr. Taylor saw John walking in with the bridle and halter over his shoulder he knew what this man wanted. When John got close enough to hear Mr. Taylor said with a smile.

"Did you lose a couple of horses somewhere?"

"No" John replied, "But I came to find a couple of horses if the price is right and I like what I see."

"Well the price is right and you will like what you see because we only have the best of animals here. You must be John Mullen? Oscar was telling me in town one day you would be looking for horses in the next little while. Well you have come to the right place." was Mr. Taylors reply.

The men introduced themselves to each other and John was invited to dinner then they would talk business. The dinner was beautiful after the walk over to the farm. John thanked Mrs Taylor and the men went out to the barn to tend to business.

Mr. Taylor said he had four of five horses he was willing to sell. When he found out that John wanted two horses for all around farm work and maybe some road work he said he had just the team for him.

The men went out to a large corral behind the barn. There were about fifteen to twenty horses in the corral. John noticed that some of the mares were in foal and didn't have too long to go before dropping a foal. He asked it any of the mares were for sale.

"No", replied Mr. Taylor, "I would not sell them now when they are so close to having their foals, but maybe in the fall I will sell you one that would bring you a foal next spring".

John said, "He thought that would be the answer and he would be very pleased if he could buy one of the mares in the fall.

With this Mr. Taylor pointed to a pair of bay geldings that were drinking from the water trough. I think those two would make a good team for you he said, they are about the same size and would make a good strong team. They have both been broken for every kind of work that you can think of that would be needed around the farm. They are mostly Percheron with a bit of Belgian in them. You can ride either one of them but the closest one is the most quiet to ride. He is called Shorty and is seven years old. The other one is a little more spirited and is five years old. His name is Claire.

John looked at the horses and was pleased with what he saw. They looked like just what he wanted. He hoped the price was not too high because he would be proud to own this team for himself. He asked what the price would be. When Mr. Taylor told it was a bit higher than he wanted to go but they were a very good looking team and also he was promised a good deal on a mare in the fall if he bought this team. John agreed to the price and the deal was settled. They caught the two horses and John put the bridle on Shorty and the halter on Claire said goodbye to Mr. Taylor then jumped up onto Shorty's back and headed for home. Claire led very good behind the other horse so they made good time on the road.

When they got to Ethelton John stopped in to see Mike to see if he knew of any farm equipment for sale. Mike told John that he had a good wagon and box he had just fixed up and also a one shear plow that would be good for what John would need for putting in the garden. He also had some other equipment like harrows and a small disc that he would sell for a good price. They made a deal on the equipment and John said he would pick them up when his stuff arrived from Eatons. He was going to check at the station and see when the order was due.

John went over to the station and found out that his order was already there. He was so pleased it would save him another trip to pick the stuff up. He opened the boxes until he found the harness he had ordered, he then put the harness on the horses and hooked them up to the wagon. Mike sold him a tin of axle grease for the wagon and helped him load his equipment and the order from the station. Then John picked up the mail, had a little chew the rag with George and then headed home.

When John arrived at the farm he was the most proud man in the whole province. There he was with his own team and wagon, enough equipment to make a garden and a big order from Eatons. The first thing he did was yell at everyone.

"Well what do you think of this rig. It sure feel good to drive your own wagon."

Oscar walked around the wagon then said to John. "Not a bad looking team you got there. I know how you must feel right now, it wasn't too long ago that I got my first team and I was pretty damn proud to drive them home."

"Yes you were", Stella said, "I think you even swore then when you came home" She could not help but let Oscar know she had not missed what he had said.

Florence looked at the wagon and said, "Sure glad the order is in now all we need is a bed and stove and we will be able to move into our house. Stella must be getting fed up with us hanging around here in the way all the time."

"No such thing", Stella exclaimed, "We will miss you when you move, it got a little much sometimes in the winter with not enough to do, but the summer here will be work until the snow flies again."

"Anyway"' Florence said, "It will do us both good to be in our own places and get down to the business of running a homestead".

"Yes", Oscar agreed, "it was time to start running a homestead but I am sure as hell going to miss the help that John has been around here this winter".

"Well let's go have supper"' Stella added, "before Oscar really gets carried away."

This broke up the little meeting and John put his team away and went to supper.

The next day John and Florence drove over to their house. They unloaded the equipment and worked the rest of the day on the place. They also made plans to go to Melfort and get the furniture that they would need to start living in the place. They decided to do this as soon as they could.

Two days later John and Florence drove their team to Ethelton and made arrangements with Mike to look after their team for a couple of days. They were to catch the five o'clock train to Melfort, shop all the next day for what.they needed and return the next morning on the Eight o'clock train. They would stay at the Hotel there. It would give them a little bit of a holiday even if the day was going to be busy.

This was exactly what they did and the day after they returned on the train to pick up all their household supplies at the station. They tried to pay Mike for looking after the team but he would have nothing to do with any money. He explained he would get lots of work from John when he got his homestead running, anyway he had already sold him some farm equipment. A little favour between friends was all a part of living here.

They loaded up their household goods and headed for home. It would not be long now before they would be moving into their own home.

The next day everyone went over to the house to help move the new furniture. The stove was a big Burbank and was a heavy job for Oscar and John. It was all in pieces which was a good thing as it came complete with a big warming oven on top and a water reservoir at the end. This stove would be good for heating as well as cooking,

Florence and Stella put the dishes on the shelves that had been put up and the pots and pans in the cupboard that had been made out of wooden boxes with canvas hanging in front for a door. They would have to wash everything after the stove was set up and working.

Oscar told John that he would have to haul over a load of wood to keep them going until they had a chance to cut some. Also a load of oat straw to feed the horses until the fresh grass was up and they could get food for themselves.

John agreed to this and said, "Thanks Oscar that will come in handy, you know in a couple of more days we will be able to move in to this place. All I have to do is clean out the well and a few more small jobs and she will be in real ship shape condition around here."

"What the Hell". Oscar replied, "you helped cut the wood you should get some of it. Yes you won't get in too soon the soil is just about dry enough to start getting ready for a garden. If you move some of that manure up from the barn you should be able to make things grow."

The men and women worked all day and had thing in good shape by that night. They went home real tired and were not long heading to bed that night.

On the following Sunday Florence and John moved into their own house. They were really pleased to be alone in the little place. When they were getting ready for bed that night Florence said to John.

"It took a long time but we are finally in our own house."

"Yes", John said, "we have worked hard this last while, we have moved into our own house and have seen our first spring break-up."

CHAPTER 7

Spring Work and Fun

The warm weather and bright sunny days soon had the grass turning green and the trees coming out in leaf. It was time to plow some land for a garden. With the one shear plow and the team of horses John started to turn the soil over.

John had not had a lot of experience with the plowing so there were a few times when he ran into problems. When he figured out that if he tied the reins together and put them over one shoulder and under the other arm he could hold onto the plow with both hands. If the horsed needed to be steered then he could do this with one hand and hold onto the plow with the other one.

Things started to go along really good after the first few hours of plowing. Now even the rows were starting to look straight and not like a crooked trail of a snake. One think John didn't know about was rocks.

In the middle of the afternoon Florence was bringing a cold drink and a sandwich out to John when he had his first run in with a rock.

The plow hooked into a good sized rock and the team feeling the load tighten leaned into the harness even harder. John flew up over the plow handles and landed on his back in the new plowed dirt. As he landed he yelled "whoa" and the team stopped. As he went to get up Florence said,

"Are you alright? gosh you looked like the man on the flying trapeze."

"Jesus H Christ" John hollered, "a man could break his bloody neck doing that. Yes I am O.K. It is a good thing I landed on the new plowed soil it is a lot softer than what hasn't been plowed yet. You would come along and see this wouldn't you!"

Florence could hardly keep the grin from her face it had looked so funny and no harm was done except for a little hurt pride. So with a straight face she said to John. "You were doing so good and it is so warm I thought I would bring you out a cold drink and a sandwich. But I didn't expect you to turn cartwheels for me. I guess we will have to get Stella over to wash your mouth out with soap."

With this they both had a good laugh. John sat down to have his drink and sandwich. He told Florence that he would have enough plowed by night for the garden. Tomorrow he would disc and harrow the plot then it would be ready for planting. It would be about two acres and would give them a good supply for the winter. He said that he would go to Pathlow and get some seed and also go see Mr. Dahl about the papers for their homestead. Pathlow was only about six miles to the East and it would be good to buy supplies from different places and see some different people. Anyway the Hotel there might even sell him a beer if it was a hot day.

Florence looked at him and said, "That is probably the biggest reason but it would be a good idea to see what was there for shopping. The train runs from there to Regina and at Ethelton it runs to Saskatoon."

A couple of days later John went to Pathlow to pick up the seeds. He got potatoes, turnip, carrots, cabbage, parsnip, corn, peas and beans. Much of this they could put in the root cellar and use it over the winter.

Florence and John spent the next while planting the garden then they hoped for a rain storm. It would sure help the seeds get a good start if it rained and then there was some more warm weather.

For the next while John plowed up a small clear spot on the side of a hill by the house. He would plant some clover and timothy mix for the horses this winter. He would have to see about getting a cow so they could have milk and make butter. Now they had to go over to Oscar's to get milk and in this warm weather it didn't keep too long even though they kept it down the well where it was cooler. But the cows would have to wait for a while until he could make some money. He could not even plant anything on his own place because it was all trees except for about a acre. Maybe he would build their house there. It sure would be nice if he could get a job working on the road with his team.

John spent the next while fixing up a few things around the place and cutting wood and sawing it up with a buck saw. He would split the wood so it would be dry for the winter. For now he would pick out old dry dead trees. They sure were hard work but you couldn't use green wood in a stove. They didn't need the stove for heat but they had to cook and heat water for washing, cooking and many other things.

Florence was kept busy with the cooking, washing, weeding the garden, picking wild strawberries, looking after the dozen chickens they had bought. It sure was nice to have fresh eggs to eat and to cook with. She was making strawberry jam and it sure was hot working over the wood stove at this time of year. The days seemed so long it never got dark until about eleven o'clock at night and it was daylight at four o'clock in the morning. The weather was really warm now and it did not cool off to much at night. The mosquitos were real bad now especially just after supper in the evening. They seemed to be able to get in anywhere and the windows had to be open to try and let in a little breeze, they would have to get some screening someday.

One day Oscar dropped in to see Florence and John. He said it was nice to see they had a garden coming along and that they had chickens. It looked like they would make out in the long run.

John said, "Yes things are starting to come along but it would be nice if he could get a little work to help pay for some of the things that they would need. We should have a cow, and the pension cheque will not take care of every thing"

"Well", Oscar said, "I then have two good pieces of news for you. First next Thursday is July the first and we like to have a few people in to enjoy the holiday. Come over right after dinner and we can spend the afternoon having a little fun. Then we will have some roast chicken for supper and make some ice cream before all my ice is gone."

"God that sounds good" John said, "it has been so long since we have had ice cream that I forget what it tastes like. That will be really nice."

Florence added, "That does sound good Oscar. But I think we will come over before dinner and bring a lunch, nothing fancy just some home made bread, fresh strawberry jam, and a few other thing I can scrape up. Then I can help Stella prepare the supper. Who else will be coming?"

"Oh just the Cosman's and maybe the Walter Campbell family. We should have a good get together. Darn it I nearly forgot the other news. They are looking for men and teams to work on the forty four trail roadway. It will not be to close to home but Florence can come and stay with us if she doesn't want to stay alone. This may help you out getting some more of the things you will need."

John said, "I will sure look into that and we will sure be over next Thursday."

"O.K. great", Oscar replied, "we will be expecting you and I better get going because I have a lot of work to do."

With this they said goodbye to each other and then carried on with their work.

On Thursday John and Florence arrived at Oscar's place. Stella had already plucked and cleaned the chickens that Oscar had killed that morning. They had lunch and then the women started to prepare things for supper. They made cream puffs that would be filled with whipped cream, stuffing for the chickens and many vegetables had to be washed and cleaned. The other company arrived and one of the women brought a couple of strawberry pies, and another women brought some rhubarb pies. It looked like it would be a real good feast for everyone. While the women were doing all the work the men were having a good time. They had got Oscar's small 22 rifle and were doing some shooting behind the barn. One of the men had brought a small bottle of Brandy so they had a few shots of that just to celebrate the first of July. The afternoon went by very fast and before they knew it Stella was calling them for supper.

It was a great meal and when they had finished the main course the women cleared off the table while the men turned the ice cream maker out on the porch. It wasn't too long before the ice cream was ready and they sat down again to have dessert. They were all so full they could hardly move. The women cleaned up the dishes while the men sat and talked and some enjoyed a smoke.

They all thanked Stella for the wonderful meal then headed off to their respective homes.

On the way home John said to Florence, "That sure was a nice day. I have never had so much to eat in my life."

Florence's reply was, "I noticed that and I have never worked so hard to get a meal ready, but Stella sure knows how to cook a good meal. I have learned a lot of thing from her."

So they both agreed that even with so much hard work you can still have a little fun but you have to work hard to enjoy it.

CHAPTER 8

Summer 1920

On the second of July John went to Flett Springs to see if he could get some work for himself and his team on the forty four trail road. It was about a three hour drive in the wagon but that was fine because he had taken a lunch and some feed for the team. When he arrived at the municipal hall he tied his team to the hitching rail and went inside to see about work.

The clerk there told him that the road foreman would be in soon and John could have a talk with him. John thanked him very much and went outside to wait in the shade of a big poplar tree at the side of the building. He rolled himself a smoke and just sat there enjoying the rest.

It wasn't too long before a man drove up in a buggy and went into the office. He then came outside and came over to talk with John. He shook hands with John and said.

"Hello John, the clerk told me you would be here and that you are looking for work on the road. My name is Fred Banks and I am the foreman on the job. Is that your team over there?"

"Yes", John replied, "That is my team and wagon over there."

"That is a fine looking team and they look like they could handle road work". Fred stated.

John looked pleased and answered, "Yes when I bought them from Mr. Taylor he said they would be good for road work."

"Well", Fred nodded and said, "if you got them from Mr. Taylor then they will be good horses. Now that we have established that the horses will be O.K. for the work, how about you? We will want you to work from Monday morning until Saturday night. If the weather is good you will work some very long days. If we have rain the extra hours will help make up for the time you may lose. We always stop at five on Saturdays to give you a chance to go home for Sunday. We start work on Mondays at Eight so you can leave home that morning before work. Most of the workers live within a two or three hour drive from here. The other days we work from six in the morning till six at night. We supply the feed for the horses and you eat breakfast and supper at the camp. Dinner time meals are brought out to you on the job. The bunk houses and eating house move right along with the road work. They are on wheels so you will not have far to go back and forth. You are expected to look after your own team and harness, we will supply the equipment. That is about all I can think of that you should know. Maybe after you think that over you may not want to become a road worker."

John did not think very long before he replied, "Oh yes I want to work on your road, I have to get a few dollars together to help get my wife and I through the winter. When would you like me to start?"

Fred smiled and said. "How about Monday morning, that will give you a couple of days to clean up things around home and the likes. Will your wife be alright by herself or have you made plans for that?"

"Oh we can look after that alright, she has a brother that lives only a couple of miles away and she can go there if she does not like staying alone. I will be here Monday morning, do you want me to bring the wagon?" was John reply.

"Yes, good idea," Fred replied. "we may start you hauling some gravel from the Pleasant Valley Station until you have a chance to see how the men work the scoops or slushers as they are called. We will give you extra for the use of your wagon.

The men talked over the expected payment for work then shook hands and agreed to meet at the road construction on Monday morning.

John's team had been eating the straw that he had brought with him and were ready to hit the road. He started down the road eating his dinner and thinking about all the things he would have to do in the next couple of days. A man had a lot of time to think when driving a wagon for the horses would follow the road and did not travel too fast. He would have a lot of smokes and thoughts before he reached home.

When John got home he told Florence what had happened. She did not let on that she was not looking forward to staying alone, but she did not have much else of a choice for they needed the money to buy a cow and get into a better house before the winter. This one with just tar paper on the walls sure would not do in a Saskatchewan winter. The pension cheque would help buy their food but that was about all until they could make and grow more of their own.

John said they would go to Pathlow in the morning and buy what they needed for he would not have much of a chance to go to town unless it rained a lot and they could not work on the road. It looked like he would be able to work on the road until harvest time and then he could get on with a harvest crew. They talked over the many things they would have to get in town. John said they were going to Pathlow because it had a hardware store and he needed some leather for harness repairs and he also was going to buy Florence a 22 rifle, he would show her how to use it on Sunday.

Florence looked at him with that what are you talking about look and said, "What do you think will happen, the Indians have been friendly for years?"

"Well", John answered, "that one hen has young chicks and the Hawks may bother them. If you take a few shots at them they may stay away from here. Anyway it might make you feel better."

The next couple of days John and Florence were busy as beavers. They even cut a bit of hay in the little plot by the house and left it to dry and Florence would rake it up in piles when it got dry. They had a little target practice with the little Belgian single shot 22 that John had bought. He was surprised at how quick Florence had caught on to using the gun.

On Monday morning they said goodbye to each other and John was on his way to work on the road. Florence watched him drive down the road, then sighed and said to herself, "its only five o'clock so I guess I had better find something to do. What a lonely place I had better keep busy.

Everything went well with the road work for John. He had people to talk with at night after supper but it was very lonely for Florence back on the homestead.

One day while Florence was working in the kitchen making Saskatoon jam she heard the chickens making a fuss out side. She looked out the window and muttered "that damn hawk is back again maybe I should take a shot at it with the rifle." She picked up the rifle from behind the door and stepped outside. The hawk was just coming in over the chickens in a low swoop Florence lifted up the gun and let fly at the hawk. The Hawk did a loop in the air and then fell to the ground. A mans voice spoke from the driveway and scared the hell out of Florence.

He said, "Lady I have seen good shooting before but if that ain't all, and with just a 22 rifle. I hunt and trap for a living and have never seen anything like that before. I will go and get rid of the Hawk for you."

With that he got off his horse and took care of the dead Hawk. Florence thought to her self, he looks like a half breed he will probably keep the tail feathers and sell them to some Indian tribe. She also wondered what she would do now.

The man came back and said to Florence. "My name is Jimmy and I live on the old Lambert place west of here. You must be Mrs Mullen and I am pleased to meet you. I am always happy to meet good rifle shooters. Could I water my horse at your well for I still have a few miles to go?'

"Yes of course", she said, "Just call me Florence and maybe you would like a cup of tea and some Saskatoon jam?"

"I would be very pleased" Jimmy replied, "I will just water my horse and let him pick at some grass. I knew that smell meant you were cooking something good."

Florence thought to herself what have I done now. Me alone and asking a half-breed to eat with me. But it is so lonely here and maybe after he saw the way I blew that Hawk out of the sky he will think twice before he would try anything. She then realized she still had the gun in her hand. She put a shell in the gun and put it behind the door.

Jimmy came back and Florence asked him to come inside and have the tea and sandwich. He said he would sit out on the step if she didn't mind. She was happy about his suggestion and brought his snack to him. He ate the food and got up to leave. He turned to Florence and said.

"Thank you very much for the food, I was getting very hungry. You make very good bread and jam. Thank you again."

With this Jimmy went to his horse and was on his way. Florence was glad to see him go but had been glad to hear another human voice other than her own for a change.

The next time John came home she told him about the Hawk and they both had a good laugh. John looked at her and said. "You with your Hawk and me with my Partridge we will be known as the sharp shooters of the Carrot River valley. If only they knew how lucky we both were."

Florence replied, "Well if you don't tell neither will I, it might not hurt if people don't know the difference."

"It's a deal", John said, "maybe the reputation will make you feel better when you are alone here."

The summer went by quickly with John only having Sundays to work at home and Florence canning wild berries and everything she could from the garden. By the third week of August John was home from the road work and would now have to look for a job with a harvest crew.

John and Florence were pleased that it had been a good summer. They had some food away for winter and a few extra dollars to spend. All in all it had been a good first summer on the Homestead.

CHAPTER 9

Fall 1920

It wasn't long before John got jobs helping with the harvest. At first he was putting the sheaves up into stooks. These were the bundles of grain that had been left by the binder and had to be put up into upright piles to dry. It was hard hot work and impossible to keep up to the binder, so you worked late some times.

Some of the places were close enough for John to get home at night but this made for a early rise in the morning so he could start work as early as light would allow and there was no dampness on the grain.

One day there was a light rain so no crops could be cut for a couple of days. John was told if he made a rack for his wagon he could work with a threshing crew, he would make more money with having a team than just being a field pitcher. John thought this was a good idea. Also he had made a deal that he would take most of his pay in grain, straw and hay. It would be a long winter and he would need this to feed his horses and chickens. He also wanted to get a cow and a pig or two if he could.

While John was working helping other farmers with the harvest, Florence was canning corn, digging potatoes, parsnips, carrots, turnips and storing them in the cellar. They would be safe there in case they had a early frost. They would have to be moved again when they found another house to spend the winter,

One night when John came home he told Florence that he had some good news. He said he had been talking with Walter and he said his brother would not be here for the winter. He was leaving right after the crops were off, and we could stay at Harry's place for the winter. It was just a small house but would do fine for just two persons. Harry is a bachelor so did not build too big a place. There is a good barn and chicken coop. Walter is going to look after the stock so we can use the outbuildings also.

"That sounds good," Florence replied, "but what will we do in the spring?"

"I think we can come back here in the spring," was Johns reply, "and if I cut logs on our homestead this winter and have them squared off at Mikes, I will be able to work on our own place."

Florence looked at John and said, "Let's just take one step at a time, everything has worked out not too bad so far. It sure would be nice to get into our own place some day."

John kept working harvesting until late in September. Florence kept on canning for the winter. Some of the chicks were full grown by now and a few of the roosters were killed and preserved. This way they could be eaten later and they would not have to be fed in the meantime. Florence was getting good at canning in the glass jars. She had asked a lot of questions of different people and they had been a great help to her. Now as long as they did not get poisoned over the winter everything would be just fine.

Now that the harvest was over John and Florence started moving into their winter home. The place was nice and clean so not much had to be done to get the place ready. They only had to move the small things as the stoves and main furniture were already there. It would not take too much time to make the move.

When they had moved the chickens and hauled over most of

the wood the move was about completed. John said he was going to town to see if he could get some news on where he could buy a cow, so they could have fresh milk this winter. maybe even a pig or two if the price was right.

Florence said she would like to go with him to get some supplies that she would need in the next while. They agreed they would go the next day.

They started bright and early the next morning. The air was cool now in the morning. The leaves on the trees were most beautiful with each kind showing its bright colours. There was a bright red on some trees, some were orange and some were yellow. This made a real nice mix of colours and Florence could not help but say.

"This must be the best time of the year in this part of the country. The trees are very pretty, the days are not too hot and all of the bugs are gone. I wish it would be like this all year."

"Yes", John replied, "from the middle of August to October are sure nice. But you know the snow can fly any time now."

They rode on in silence just enjoying the nice weather and the fall trees. It wasn't too long and they were pulling into Ethelton and tied the team up in front of the store.

John said he would go over and see Mike and find out where he could get a cow and would meet Florence at the store later.

Mike greeted John with a big smile and said, "What can I do for you today?"

John answered, "maybe you can tell me were I can but a cow or two for not too much money and maybe a pig or two?"

Mike stood thinking for a minute then said to John' "You may be able to pick up a cow or two at the Paterson farm about a mile south of here. And just before you get to the Paterson place Bart Ford has a quarter section. He might sell you a couple of pigs. They are good people and will sell at a fair price."

John thanked Mike and then went over to the Post Office to get the mail. His pension cheque was there so he would have a little more cash to buy what he needed.

When he got to the store Florence had picked out most of what they needed and was just talking to Mrs Boyd the store owner.

John said, "Hello Mrs Boyd can you cash my pension cheque for me to-day?"

"Sure John", she replied, "I will do that any time I can. Most of it is used up here anyway, sooner or later,"

"I guess you're right," John laughed, "but this time I want to take most of it with me."

"That's fine, I have been enjoying talking to your wife. She doesn't get into town very often." was the reply, "You should bring her in more often."

"Yes", John said, "if I get a caboose built this winter we will be able to come to town more often. But with the road work and harvest we have not had much time for anything else."

With this they finished their business at the store and went out to the wagon. After they had started to leave town John told Florence about what Mike had told him. It was only about a mile to the Ford farm so they got there in no time.

Mr. Ford came out to meet them from the barn. His wife came out from the house. The black and white mutt of a dog gave a couple of barks and went and laid down under the porch.

Mr. Ford said, "Good morning, , what can I do for you good folks?"

John replied, "Good morning, I am John Mullen and this is my wife Florence. We have come to see if you have a couple of pigs for sale?"

Mr. Ford answered with, "I'm Bart and this is my wife Dora, you must know our last name if you found the place."

Dora spoke up and said, "Florence you get down off that wagon and come in the house and we can have a good talk before you have dinner with us. The men can talk about pigs if they want to but we can talk about more interesting things."

Florence was quick to reply. "Thank you but we didn't come for dinner and we have to go over to the Paterson place to see about a cow. Thank you very much it was a real nice offer."

"Well the Paterson place is only a quarter of a mile over there," Dora pointed across the field, "and you certainly will have dinner with us. And the men can go over to the Paterson place after dinner while you stay here. It is not often that we get visitors and both Bart and I have been wanting to meet you people. Anyway Bart and Jack Paterson are good friends and he can maybe help John get a good buy on some cows. So now that we have settled that let's get in the house and get to know each other.'

The women went in the house and the men went out to the barns and pig pens. Bart showed John a sow and a boar that he would sell. He would be able to breed the sow and raise some pigs of his own. The price was right so they made a deal. Bart suggested to John that they leave the pigs until after going over to the Paterson's, then they could come back here and load them in the wagon. John agreed, so both men wandered up to the house for dinner.

During dinner the men re-fought the war as Bart had been in Infantry and John had been in the Artillery. Bart had been wounded in the leg with shrapnel and still limped a bit. John had been gassed and had only one good lung. They both got pensions and had also fought in most of thee major battles. The women talked about just about everything from canning to where they had come from before moving out here.

After a good dinner the men went over to the Paterson place to try and buy cows. They were only gone about a hour and half when they returned with two cows tied behind the wagon. They loaded the two pigs into the wagon and then went up to the house.

Dora and Florence were still talking and did not even hear the men cone in. So Bart said.

"Well I think they must be getting along just fine. They were so busy chewing the rag that they didn't even hear us come in. What have you women been cooking up since we left after dinner.?"

"Now Bart," Dora said, "We have not been cooking up anything. But we have decided that John and Florence will come to our place for Christmas and we will go to their place for New Years. We will start before dinner and stay the whole day, that way we can have a real good visit. You two men can fight the whole war over again and maybe you won't get hurt this time."

Every one laughed and Bart said, "I knew you would be up to something and I think that it sounds real good. We have found some good friends here and we have so much in common. I think it would be a good idea if on November the eleventh I drop you off at the Mullen's place and John a I go to Pathlow to observe Remembrance Day."

"That sounds like a good idea," Dora replied, "if Florence will have me for the whole day. If I know anything about observing Remembrance Day you had better make arrangements for Jack to milk your cows that night and the next morning because you will probably be in no shape to come home that night."

Every one had a good laugh at that and Florence said. "That sounds good Dora but if the men come home in bad shape they can sleep in the barn, we only have one bed in the new place but we can fix up something."

Before John and Florence left they completed the arrangements for November the eleventh. Both women knew how much this meant to both of the men and anyway it would give them a chance to get to know each other better.

Bart told John that if he cut across his farm at a forty five degree angle there was a gate in the fence he could go through and if he continued the same way through the next farm he would come out on the road he had used to go to Ethelton and he would cut off about three miles of travel. Just make sure the gates were left closed so any livestock could not get out.

John thanked Bart for his help and Dora for the nice dinner. Then with hand shakes all around and goodbyes John and Florence were on their way.

They travelled on for while both tied up in their own thought. Finally John said. "This sure has been a nice day. we have two cows, one that is milking now and one that will freshen in the early spring. We have two pigs that should breed and start us on the way to raising some of our own pork."

"Yes John it has been a good day" Florence replied, "and don't forget we have also made two very nice friends. We are very lucky to have met a couple that both of us like. I think we will have many good times together over the years to come.'

CHAPTER 10

First Prairie Christmas

The first week of November was nice clear weather. The days were bright and warm and the nights were cool.

John was kept busy hauling wheat and oat straw for bedding and feed for the stock. Florence was working on a feather blanket to use when it got cold this winter.

When November the eleventh came around it was a nice clear day. Bart and Dora showed up early in the morning. John said he would take his team to Pathlow and give Bart's team a rest. They left right away so they could be there by eleven o'clock. The two women went into the house and were lost in their chatter.

The day went by quickly with Bart and John going to the hotel after the little ceremony at eleven. They were going to have a few beer's with some of the other vets and then head home.

Florence and Dora talked about just about everything. They made a big supper in case the men came back in time. It was about five when they heard a team coming up the road and two men singing old war songs. Dora said to Florence.

"Here come our two hero's now I'll bet they haven't had anything to eat since breakfast. It is a good thing we made a big supper."

"That's for sure" Florence replied, "they will be starved by now. I am surprised that they got back this early."

The men put the team in the barn and came up to the house. When they smelled the supper they both said at the same time. "Boy that smells good we are so hungry we could eat a horse."

The women laughed and Florence said. "Well horses are too valuable to eat so you are going to have to be happy with a little chicken."

They all sat down at the table and it wasn't long before most of the food was gone. Bart said they would leave for home soon. The road would be easy to see as there was a big moon out. Jack said he would milk the cows if he did not see a light on at our place by eight. We should make it by then.

"Yes", John said, "you will have had a long day by the time you get finished. I hope everyone had enjoyed themselves as I have? It is nice to have a day off once in a while and just have a little fun."

The Fords left for home and said they would see each other at Christmas if not before.

A few days later there was a good snow fall and the weather started to get much colder. John started to cut trees on their homestead by the little clearing above a creek. There were some nice size trees there and it was where they had chosen to build their house in the summer. The dead dry trees he hauled home at night to cut up for fire wood, with the colder weather the little wood he had left from last year was going fast. The small green trees he piled up in the clearing to make ready for a wood bee later on. This year he would be one of the places that everyone stopped. They would need dry wood for next winter and it was a good way of clearing some of the land. The bigger trees were put in a different spot and would be hauled to Mikes before spring breakup and squared for the walls of the house. Some of them would be cut into lumber for the roof and floors. He would have to make a lot of trips to get everything needed to build the house.

One night when John and Florence were sitting by the fire and reading a paper, Florence looked up at John and said, "When you build that house it might be smart to have more than one bedroom as I think there will be three of us in the family pretty soon."

John dropped the paper on his lap and exclaimed, "My God Flossie do you mean you are going to have a baby?"

Florence grinned and said, "Does that mean your happy or sad. It's hard to tell when you talk like that."

"Of course I'm happy" John replied, "good heavens woman I'm as pleased as punch. When do you expect it will happen?"

"Oh it will happen when it is ready" she answered, "probably in May sometime. Just in time to help with the spring planting."

John laughed and said, "I don't think it will be ready to help with the spring planting and I don't think you will be either."

Florence smiled and said, "We will see when the time comes. Dora is going to have a baby at about the same time."

"Gosh, John sputtered, "Bart will be pleased too. You women will really have things to talk about now. I bet you didn't tell Bart and I sooner because you figured we would go out and celebrate or something like that?"

"Yes you might be right there" she replied, "Christmas isn't far away you can celebrate then if you are so inclined."

Time went by fast and the next thing it was Christmas time and Florence and John were up early to get the chores done and leave for Fords to celebrate. John had made a small caboose with some lumber and canvas. He had mounted it on a sleigh that he had made with some of the Birch trees that grew on the homestead. It was not a professional job but would do quite well for them to travel in. The little stove would keep them warm and they could travel in comfort.

They arrived at Fords about eleven and the smell of turkey cooking was just about too much to stand. Florence said to Dora.

"Merry Christmas, my gosh you must have been up at four o'clock to have that bird just about ready for dinner?"

Dora replied, "Merry Christmas to you Florence and John. Yes I was up pretty early but if we are to have anything left for supper it had to be a nice sized bird."

"It sure is a big turkey," Florence answered, "this cold weather gives one a good appetite so I don't think there will be much left of that one."

It wasn't long before they had all eaten so much they could hardly move. Dora was grinning when she said. "Florence if we eat any more the men will be going for nurse Trail because they will think that we are ready to give birth right now."

Everyone had a good laugh about that. The men went into the living room and started to play crib by the big heater. The women did up the dishes and came in to join them for a few hands. There was a lot of fun and good joking that went on between them. After working so hard on their homesteads it was nice to see them enjoying each others company so much.

In the middle of the afternoon John said, "I have to take a walk so I can work up a appetite for supper. Do you want to come Bart?"

"Sure", Bart answered, "it will do us good to walk around for a while. My old leg gets stiff if I sit too long. I guess it must be that Heinie shrapnel gets cold in the winter and shrinks up. How about your lungs John do they bother you in the cold weather?"

"Oh sometimes when it is real cold", John said, "I can feel my chest tighten up a bit. But if I breath through a scarf or something like that it isn't too bad."

The men put on their heavy jackets and boots and went for a walk out toward the barn. When they got to the barn they went inside. Bart turned to John and said.

"I think it's time we had a little drink to celebrate Christmas and the addition to our families."

"Sounds like a good idea," John replied, "a baby will sure change things around the home won't it Bart?"

The men had a drink from a bottle that Bart had hidden in the barn. They talked for a while and then went back to the house. They played some more cards and then enjoyed another good meal for supper.

After the kitchen was cleaned up Florence and John got ready to head home. They said goodbye, thanked each other for the small presents they had given each other. They promised to see each other again when the Fords came over for New Years.

Work went on as usual except for the break for New Years. It was much the same as Christmas with two big meals and the men taking a walk in the afternoon so they could have a drink to celebrate New Years. The two holidays had been a nice time for both families, it only made them closer together and they decided to meet as often as they could to visit.

The next couple of months went by fast. The weather was very cold at times. John cut as much wood and trees for lumber as the weather would permit. Florence kept busy with the house work and now she was making baby clothes for the coming event.

John got his logs hauled to Mikes, cut into lumber and hauled back to the clearing where he was to build the house. The spring breakup was not too far away now. They would have to move back to the house that they stayed in last summer. Florence was quite big now and it was hard for her to do the chores. He would have to stick close to home in case he had to go and get nurse Trail in a hurry. It was about seven miles to the nurse's place so that would take a couple of hours if the roads were good, at this time of year they could be in real bad shape.

The winter had not been too bad this year. All the stock had survived fine. It looked like there would be some more pigs and one of the cows was going to freshen any time. He would have to go and get the mare that Mr. Taylor had kept all winter. They had thought it best if she stayed there. John had paid more for her but she had been looked after all winter because he did not have a lot of feed. He would wait until after the baby was born before he went to pick her up.

All in all the winter had passed quickly and with the break at Christmas and New Years it had helped them forget for a while about the long winters. They missed the rest of the family back east but had received a few letters and had kept up with the news of the world with their magazines. If one could keep busy “which was not hard to do on a homestead” time just seemed to slip by.

They were both looking forward to spring and the starting of their new family.

CHAPTER 11

Lots Of New Faces

The move back to the new house at the first of May went off without a hitch. Florence was very big now and could not help very much, but she was still there and doing whatever she could.

When they were going over with their last load of things John said to Florence. "You know this bumping along in the wagon might not be to good for you? Maybe we should have a buggy as they ride a little easier. I hear old Alex has one for sale and he only lives a couple of miles away so I might slip over to-morrow and see what he wants for it. If I have to go for nurse Trail it would be faster and better than this wagon.

Florence replied, "Yes the wagon is quite rough but maybe it will speed things along and I won't be the size of a house any more."

John laughed and said, "You know a lot of things on our homestead are big right now. What with our new mare Queen ready to foal, the sow going to have a litter and old Bossy the cow going to calf we may have a population explosion around this place."

Florence gave John a look that told him he had said something wrong, then she said.

"I don't think I like being lumped in with the livestock! But you are right there is going to be a big increase around here this spring.

John did not say any more, he figured he was close enough to being in trouble as it was and he did not want to upset Florence right now.

The next day John went over to see Alex Mann about buying the buggy. Alex was a war veteran also and had been wounded in the stomach when in France. He could not do much heavy work but got by on his pension and by renting his to other farmers for a percentage of the crops.

Alex was glad to see John and they had a little chin wag for a while. Then John said.

"I can't stay too long as my wife is ready to give birth any day. I heard you had a buggy for sale and wondered if I could buy it from you?"

"Yes", Alex said, "I have a two seat buggy that I don't use any more as I have a one seater that is good enough for me just to go back and forth to town with. I don't want much for it and if you need to use it now you can pay me when you can. In fact I would rather trade something for it that I might get more use of than money."

John replied, ""I haven't got much to trade right now but my sow is going to have pigs soon. Would a couple of them do as a payment?"

"I'll tell you what John, if you throw in a batch of your wives home made bread and some fresh butter it is a deal. You know us bachelors don't like eating our own cooking all the time."

John reached out and shook Allex's hand and said, "That's a deal as soon as the wife is back to that kind of work I will bring over two pigs and the food you asked for. Can we tie the buggy behind the wagon so I can tow it home?'

"Don't see any reason why not was the reply it will save you coming back to get it later."

When John pulled into the yard Florence yelled at him from the window. "You look like a train coming in here. I am glad you got the buggy as I think the time is getting close."

"Yes I am glad too", John answered, "do you want me to go and get nurse Trail now?"

"Heavens no, "Florence exclaimed,. "I said close not ready."

"Oh that's good," John sighed with relief, "anyway I made a good deal for the buggy. Just two pigs when they are weaned and some bread and butter from you."

"That sounds good, I hope you can keep up your end of the bargain. I know I can after I get rid of this big stomach. Well it won't be long now so don't put the buggy away too far."

The next morning after breakfast Florence said to John. "I think you had better go and get nurse Trail, you won't have to hurry just take your time. I know it will be a while yet. anyway I spent a year working in a hospital so everything will be just fine."

"All right ", John answered, "I will be on my way real soon. It won't take too long to make the trip as the roads are not to bad right now."

A while later John checked with Florence again and then left to pick up the nurse. It would take better than two hours if everything went right. She would have to pack a few things. He hoped that she was home and not playing midwife some other place.

John got back with the nurse just before noon. By this time Florence was in some pain and was glad to see the nurse. Miss Trail had worked in a hospital for years but now was semi-retired and just helped with women who were having babies. she was very good and everyone around called on her at time of birth.

Nurse Trail turned to John and said. "John you keep a good fire going and keep out of the way. If we need you we will call. Florence and I will be in the bedroom and it would help if you looked after the meals for us. Don't worry it takes a long time for the first baby to come."

"O.K." John replied, "just holler if you want me to do anything.

I will only go to the barn when it is time to do the chores. The rest of the time I will be close by and I will look after the meals and keep the fire going and lot's of hot water on the stove."

The afternoon went by then dinner time. John went out and did the chores in record time and then was back at the house in case he was needed. It was still light outside at this time of year so he sat on the back step and tried to read the paper. The words did not make much sense as he had his mind on what was going on in the house. Just before dark nurse Trail came out side and said to John.

"You may as well go in and try and sleep on the couch we will let you know if anything happens."

John said, "It will be hard to go to sleep but I will give it a try."

It was some time later John had gone to sleep and the next thing he knew the nurse was telling him to wake up. He jumped off the couch, still in his clothes and asked. "What's the matter is everything alright?"

"Oh yes everything is just fine." the nurse replied, "you better come in and see Florence now she has something to show you."

John leapt into the bedroom and saw Florence laying on the bed with a little bundle beside her. He said, "You have had the baby is everything O.K."

In a tired voice Florence said. "Yes everything is fine. We have a baby girl and she is just fine."

"But I slept right through the whole thing," John exclaimed, "You should have let me know."

The nurse laughed and said, "We thought you would be a better help sleeping and Florence said you never hear anything once you have gone to sleep. Now you had better let Florence sleep for she has been through a fair time. You can see her and the baby in the morning."

John said, "O.K. I guess we will call her Helen Phyllis like we planned if it was a girl. He patted Florence's hand and smiled at her.

As he was going out the door they heard him mumble to himself. "Big bloody help I was, I slept through the whole thing."

The nurse stayed around for about ten days. It was a good thing as John had gone to Pathlow to register the birth at the municipal office. He was pretty proud and told everyone in town about his daughter Helen.

The rest of the time John was kept hopping. The sow had a litter of nine pigs and they seemed to be doing good. He would have seven left after he gave two to Alex.

The next day he was up all night while Queen gave birth to a nice little stallion colt. He was so cute and he decided to call him King. What else his mother was Queen. After everything was cleaned up John went into the house and announced that they now had four horses. Queen had just had a colt and he was going to call it King.

"My", nurse Trail said, "you sure are having a jump in population around here. What will happen next?"

Florence had just come out of the bedroom with Helen in her arms, she sat down at the table and said, "Well you have named the colt do I get to name the calf that Gertie is going to have.?"

"Sure", John said, "that is only fair you better start thinking as it could happpen any day. How is our little girl doing? I have been so busy out in the barn that I haven't had much chance to see her lately."

"She is doing fine", was the reply. "You had better have some breakfast and then rest some. You have been up all night."

"Everything is good. I have to check on Gertie soon and see how she is. I may have a nap later on if there is time."

After breakfast John went out to the barn to do the chores. When he got there another surprise greeted him. Old Gertie had given berth to a bull calf and everything was O.K. John just stood there then said to himself. "I'll be damned you can't turn your back around this place and something is being born!" John forgot about the chores and went running back up to the house to tell the women what had happened. They were as surprised as he had been.

Florence looked at John and said, "You sure didn't give me much time to think up a name did you? It happened so fast I guess we had better call him Lightning, what do you think of that for a name?"

"Sounds just great", John answered, "now I had better get back out and finish my work, then I will have a rest. So much had been going on around here it has made me tired."

A couple of days later John took nurse Trail home. She left instructions for him to not let Florence do to much for a while until she got her strength back. Any way she told him she thought he would be busy around home for a while looking after all the new off springs that had happened around the homestead. She also said she was waiting a call from the Fords as Dora was close to the time when her baby would come.

John stayed close to home for the next few days. Then he had to go to town and pick up some supplies. They would not only need food but the garden would have to be planted soon. The weather was just about warm enough to start plowing and planting. This was going to be one heck of a busy month.

While John was in town he was told that Dora had given berth to a son. He was happy to hear this and he bet Bart and Dora were happy also.

When John got home he told Florence the good news about Dora and her son. she said that it would be nice if they could go see the new baby and let them have a look at their baby. John agreed it would be nice but they would wait a while yet, until the travelling would not be too rough. They decided that some Sunday in June they would make the trip.

At supper time that night John said to Florence, "This has sure been one Hell of a month. First Helen is born then the sow had a litter of nine, next Queen had a foal and then Gertie had a calf. It's a little more than a body can take,"

Florence gave him that be careful what you say look and said. "I still don't like being lumped together with all the stock but I guess it has been a real productive month as far as births are concerned." she could not help but add. "the only thing you missed was you did not call me Flossie."

John laughed and winked at Florence and added. "Well if it makes you feel better I will from now on."

Florence had to get the last word in with, "You spend your energy at planting the garden and building us a new house, that would be more productive than teasing me."

CHAPTER 12

Summer and the Log House

After all the excitement in the past month it was now back to the work routine for both Florence and John. The garden was coming well, and the horses and cows could eat fresh grass so this made it easier and cheaper as no hay had to be bought.

John was working on the new house. He had dug out the small basement for storing vegetables and preserves. It had to be deep enough so it was below the frost line in winter. He had laid the floor and was now getting the squared logs ready for the walls. He would need some help to raise the logs into place but that would be later on. He also was working at clearing a couple of acres close to the new house. Most of the trees had been cleared the winter before when he had cut trees for lumber and wood.

The clearing of the stumps was hard work as he would have to hook a team of horses to the stump with a log chain, then cut the roots on the back side. The team worked well as they would lean into their harness until the stump pulled free. The constant heavy pulling was hard on harness many repairs had to be made to keep them in working order.

While all this was going on Florence would pack Helen out into the grass hills not far from where they were living and pick wild strawberries. When she had enough then it would be canning them for later. This was not a easy job with a small baby to look after and it was very tiring because all the other work still had to be done. Homesteading was not for the weak of heart.

On the third Sunday in June John and Florence hooked up Queen to the buggy and went to see Dora and Bart. John had made shafts for the buggy from small Birch poles so that one horse could pull the buggy. This gave the two horses that were working all week pulling stumps and doing other work a rest for a day. If he did not have too much to get at town he would use the buggy with one horse. Any way King would run alongside his mother so he would not get too far from his milk supply. It looked cute with him trotting beside the buggy like a great big dog.

Dora and Bart were real pleased to see their friends as it gave them a chance to show off each other's babies. The women had so much to talk about because so much had happened in the last little while. Harvey is what they had called their boy. He and Helen were laid at each end of the crib and left to sleep while the women talked and prepared dinner.

The men stayed out side and talked about how their stock was doing and many other things. Bart was glad to hear that the sow he had sold to John had given him a litter of nine. He asked John how the house building was going?

"Oh I'm getting there." John replied, "I have most of the logs ready for the walls. But I am going to need some help to lift them up after a while. I can get them up alone for the first few feet, but they will be too hard to lift when the wall gets up a ways."

"That's good" Bart said, "on July the first we will have a wall raising bee at your place. You tell Florence to get lots of food ready and I will bring Dora with me to help for the day. We should be able to get a fair crew together. We will just put up the logs and you can cut out the doors and windows afterwards. Have you got any lumber for the roof?"

"Yes" John nodded, "I have lots of lumber for that. Do you think we would get that far in one day?"

"Well if we can get a big enough crew together I don't see why not. It is light at about four in the morning and it does not get dark until about eleven at night. If we get a good start there is no reason at all why we can't at least get the rafters up. You can put the roof on alone as that is not heavy work. You can do the chinking between the logs and most of the rest yourself."

"Gee that sounds like a great idea Bart. It sure would be a great help. Now maybe I can get a few days work on the road. This building a house is expensive and the extra money would sure help".

The men were called to the house for dinner and when they got there they told the women what they had planned. Dora said right away that she would bring along a lot of food and they would plan it after lunch. They would have to feed their babies so it would be a good time to talk things over.

After dinner the men talked about what John had to do to be ready for the work bee. They also found time to play a few games of crib. Also there was some talk of the war and some of the good and bad times they had overseas.

When supper was over there was still a few hours of light left so the men and women did some more visiting. It was not very often that they had a chance to get together so they made the best of it when they could. Finally John and Florence left for home as they would still have chores to do when they got there.

On the way home Florence and John talked about how lucky they were to have such good friends. This seemed to be the way it was on the homestead. Every one seemed to look after each other and help when it was needed. They also planned to get ready for the work bee. It would be a big day but well worth every bit if it helped them get into their own house.

By the time July first rolled around everything was ready for the bee. Florence had baked strawberry pies and lots of bread. John had the logs ready for the house. The first people started to arrive at about seven in the morning. Even the people that lived some distance away would be there before eight. Bart and Dora were one of the first to show up. They must have got up in the middle of the night to have finished the morning chores and drive for a hour to get there. A couple of the men brought their wives along to help with the meals. There were about ten men in all to help with the house.

Dinner was served at the site of the new house. The women had put everything together in the back of a buggy and covered it with blankets to help keep it warm. It was about a mile to the new house but the men wouldn't care if the food was a little cold. They would be too hungry to care.

After the men had finished dinner they told the women that if they brought a lunch later in the afternoon they would work late and then come up to the house for supper. They would only need some sandwiches and something to drink. This way they could get a lot more done. The house was coming along great. They had about three quarters of the walls up and would be starting on the roof in the afternoon.

The men only stopped for a quick lunch later in the afternoon. The weather was warm and the cool lemonade the women had provided with the meat sandwiches really hit the spot.

By seven the walls were up and the rafters were in place. Now John could finish the rest of the place by himself. Everyone took one last look at the work they had done then crawled into their buggys or wagons and went to get supper. The men were so tired they just sat and enjoyed the mile ride to the farm house. When they arrived the women had another big meal ready for them. The women looked tired also. They had been cooking and working since early in the morning. When the men sat down at the big table John had put together with planks and saw horses Bart said.

"By God this has to be about the hardest I have ever worked on a day that was supposed to be a holiday. I"ll bet John is pleased with what we have done today".

Florence happened to be putting more food on the table and heard what Bart had said. She interjected, "I know that we both are more than pleased with what has happened today. We are both so lucky to have such good friends as you people. You don't know how much it means to us to look forward to moving into our own house by the fall." Florence could not say any more as she now had a big lump in her throat and was afraid that her voice would crack.

Bart could see that this had affected Florence and he was hasty to add. "We would not have it any other way. You will have lots of opportunities to repay us all in the years to come."

Everyone at the table either grunted or nodded their heads. They were so hungry and were to busy eating to get into much of a conversation. Also they had to get home and do the chores around their own place. It would be a long day before it was over.

When everyone had said their goodbyes and left for their respective homesteads, Florence and John went about their own chores. When they were finished they just sat down at the table and looked at each other. Florence was feeding the baby and John looked like he would fall asleep in the chair. Finally Florence said. "This has been one long day. But look at what has been done. The women even left some of the food they had brought. What a help they were. I could not have done the feeding all alone with the baby and all. They even showed me many things that I did not know about when you have to feed so many people".

"Yes it sure has been some day." John replied, "Day after tomorrow is Sunday maybe we can take a lunch with us and go down to the new house and spend the day. You might like that as it will get you away from these four walls for a while."

"That sounds like a good idea John. Now lets get to bed before we both fall asleep and wake up in the morning still sitting right here."

John and Florence had their little picnic on the Sunday. They enjoyed their day at the new house. They found lots to do and the day went by quite fast. Even the baby seemed to enjoy the day and was good for them.

The rest of the summer was spent with many hours of work. It was a very hot summer with a few big thunder and lighting storms thrown in for good measure. Florence did not like these storms especially when she was by herself when John was working on the road. He only got home on Sunday and the rest of the time she had to look after the stock, do the gardening and pick wild berries for canning. This extra work along with looking after a baby kept her busy from daylight to dark.

John did not do too much work on the roads this summer. He borrowed a mower and rake to cut some hay back in the hills around some of the swamps. This would help keep the stock in feed this winter. He had put Bossy in with the Campbell cattle. They let their bull run with the cattle and since Bossy had dried up it was a good chance to get her bred again. This way if he could keep the two cows freshening at different times they could have milk all year around. He had also take Queen to the stallion. The sow he did not have to worry about as he still had the boar that Bart had sold him. Some young chickens had hatched so things looked like they would be just fine down the road.

By the time the crops were to be harvested John had got a lot done on the house. He had finished the roof and put in the doors and window. The house was high enough that there was room for two large bedrooms upstairs and a kitchen and living-room down stairs. The second floor was done and the stairs put in. The making of the stairs was cause for a lot of sweat and swearing. A painter John maybe but a carpenter he was not. But by the time summer was over he had learned a lot and was doing well. He had cut some small trees into quarters and Florence had helped to chink up between the logs with them. With the thickness of the walls and tar paper and boards in the inside it should be nice and warm in the winter. It would be cooler in the summer also. They had both worked very hard and had a lot to show for their efforts.

One night at dinner John said to Florence. "Well I guess I will have to start helping with the harvest soon. I have to make a little money and arrange for straw and grain for the stock. I got about two acres broken this summer down by the new house but that will have to be our garden next year."

"Yes", Florence replied, "I don't like you being away from home but sometimes you are close enough to come home at night. But what else can we do? We need the money and the feed for our stock."

They both agreed that it had been a productive summer and they were looking forward to the fall when they could move into their new house.

CHAPTER 13

Harvest and the Big Gun

Before the harvest started John went to Pathlow to get some supplies. He wanted to pick up quite a bit as the next few weeks would be busy and if there was no rain then it would be a long time before he would get to town again.

When he had finished everything he had to do and was about to untie the team to head home, a man came up to him and said. "Hey there would you like to buy a good shotgun cheap. I don't need two of them and so I can let this one go. I will also throw in two boxes of shells."

John looked at the man and could tell by his accent that he was French. Probably from the next town St. Brieux. John smiled and said. "Yes I have thought about getting a shotgun so I could get a few geese and ducks when they fly south. What do you call cheap."

"Well let's say ten dollars," The man replied, "That sound good to you?"

"Five would be more like what I can afford," John stated.

The two men talked for a while and finally ended up with a deal at seven fifty. John put the gun and shells in the wagon and headed for home.

When John got home he told Florence about the shotgun and how he could shoot some geese or ducks this fall. She answered him with, “I will believe that when I see them on the table.”

The next day John went to help the other homesteaders with the harvest. He was back home for Sunday and then would be off again for a week. He was busy all day doing up the chores that he could so Florence would not have it to busy while he was away. He had been chopping up some wood by the back door and had sat down on the step to sharpen the axe. In the distance he heard the honking of geese and when he looked up he could see they were going to fly right over the house. John jumped up and reached behind the door for the shotgun. It was a big heavy gun with a very long double barrel. He shoved in two shells and stepped out into the yard. The geese were close now so John raised up the gun and pulled one trigger.

KABOOM the shot gun roared. John went flying over on his back and the gun went right over his head and landed behind him. Florence came running out of the house and yelled, “What the Hell was that?” then she turned and saw John getting up off the ground and saying.

“Jesus H Christ, that bloody thing damn nearly broke my shoulder. What the hell is it anyway a cannon?”

Florence said, “Are you all right did you break anything?”

“I’m all right “, John yelled, “but I am going to kill one Goddamn Frenchman if I ever see him again. He sure didn’t tell me that when you shot this thing it kicked like a mule.”

“I guess that’s why it was so cheap.” Florence laughed, “After all this commotion did you hit anything?.

“I don’t know” John retorted, “I was on my ass so fast that I didn’t see anything but blue sky”.

There looks like something white over there in the grass by the edge of the garden and sure enough there was a goose laying there.

John heard a noise off to his right and when he turned around there was another goose. He turned to Florence and said.

"That gun may kick a lot but it sure can knock geese out of the sky. But I will tell you one thing it won't be me who shoots it the next time."

Florence looked at John and said, "Who would buy a gun like that if it knocks you down every time you shoot it. There is no one in his right mind that would buy a gun like that."

John replied, "We won't say anything about that if I get a chance to sell it. Maybe some of the half-breeds back in the hills will buy or trade something for it. So let's just pluck the geese and say nothing to any one about that bloody big cannon."

That night for supper John and Florence had a good feed of roast goose. She would can up the rest for them to eat later on. She would have a few roosters to put up and also a lot of vegetables from the garden.

That week when John was working at the harvest with the other farmers he let it be know that he had a shotgun for sale and the price was right. No one needed one but they said that they would pass the word around.

The next Sunday when John was home for the day he was working cleaning out the barn when he heard a buggy drive up to the house. The man in the buggy saw John in front of the barn and he drove over to where he was.

"Hello Jimmy", John said, "What brings you around here today?"

"I hear you have a shotgun for sale cheap." was the reply, "could I have a look at the gun?"

John had forgotten about the shotgun and was a little surprised that the news had travelled so fast. He quickly answered. "Sure Jimmy it's up at the house. Let's go have a cup of tea and talk things over."

Jimmy tied his team up to a fence post and followed John up to the house. When they got inside Florence remembered Jimmy from the Hawk shooting. She said hello and asked him to sit down and she would get them some tea, bread and jam.

John got the gun from behind the door and showed it to Jimmy. He looked it over then asked what he would have to pay to own the gun.

The men haggled back and forth while they had their snack. John said he would throw in the shells which was only one shell short of two boxes.

They finally came to an agreement on what the price should be. Jimmy had said he had two chickens in the wagon that John could have and he would also bring him a deer tater on as full payment. The two men shook hands to seal the bargain and went outside. When they got outside Jimmy said to John.

"Maybe I should shoot this thing before I go and make sure it is O.K."

John was quick to interject, "I think the baby is sleeping and I don't think Florence would like her to be woken up now."

Jimmy said, "O.K. he would wait until later to try the gun. I will see you when I bring over the deer later in the fall."

John and Jimmy went over to the wagon and got the two chickens. They shook hands and Jimmy was on his way. John went back up to the house grinning to himself. When he got there Florence said.

"What the heck are you grinning about? I'll bet it was your quick thinking about not waking the baby if Jimmy shot off the shotgun. You weren't concerned about the baby as much as about Jimmy getting blown on his behind if he fired that gun."

John was too happy about getting rid of the gun to worry about what Florence had said. He just replied with, "Yes Flossie you might be right but two birds in the hand are worth more than a kicking shotgun. And when I get that deer we will have some meat for quite a while."

"If Jimmy shoots that gun before he shoots a deer you will be lucky not to have your behind full of buckshot. This should be very interesting indeed to say the least." was Florence's reply.

John kept working the harvest except for a few days of rain and then he worked at the house so they could move in before the cold weather came. One day when he was working with a threshing crew they had stopped for the afternoon lunch break. The men were standing around talking when Walter asked John.

"Hey John did you sell your shotgun to Jimmy?'

"Yes", John replied, "He got it about three weeks ago. Why do you ask?"

"Well from what I hear," Walter said, "old Jimmy just about killed himself with that gun. Apparently he was going home to his place and was crossing between the two swamps where the water is real close to both sides of the road. He saw three or four ducks swimming just off the side of the road. He picked up the shotgun and loaded it. Then to make sure he would get some ducks he pulled both triggers. The next thing old Jimmy knew he was in the water on the other side of the ditch. His team had run away with the buggy and were headed for home. When he crawled out of the water and up onto the road all he saw was a bunch of feathers floating on the water where the ducks had been. His shoulder was real sore and he had to walk home. He is now looking for someone to buy that gun from him."

Everyone that had heard the story were bent over laughing their heads off. They thought that was the funniest thing they had heard in a long time. John thought to himself that it wasn't too funny and some day he would meet up with Jimmy again.

When John got home he told Florence about what he had heard about the gun. She said that the gun wasn't such a good bargain after all. She then asked when they would start moving into the new house.

John said, "I will be finished working on the harvest soon. The well down by the creek below the house is working fine. A few more days work and we will be able to move in. I talked to some of the men about what I should do for a barn chicken coop and pig pen. We will need them at the new place. They said if I put up some pole frames about two feet apart and fill them with straw and put straw on the roof it would do very well for the winter. This would keep the animals warm and would be fast to build. They decided that as soon as this was done they would move into the new house.

John made good time with the buildings for the stock. The weather stayed nice and the snow held off. They got help from Florence's brother to move the heavy things like the stove. John still had to buy a heater for the winter as the cookstove would not be enough for this size of house.

After they had finished moving all the things down from the other place , they had to put up the cupboards, unpack dishes and make up a bed for the night. It was late when they were finished and sat down to have a cup of tea before going to bed.

Florence dropped into a chair, sighed and said, "You know John we are finally in our own house. We may not be making big strides but we are a little better off each year. Some day we may be able to even take off a crop of our own."

"Yes", John moaned, "we have our own house, some fine stock, and are living on our own land. The two acres that we planted into garden did very will this year. If I can ever get some more land cleared we can have a crop of grain. But at least we are eating well and things look better now than when we first came out here. I miss home sometimes and I imagine you do to, but we have been so busy working to get what we have that we even forget about that."

Florence agreed with John. They did not say any more but just crawled up the stairs to bed. It had been a busy fall and a very long tiring day. But they both looked forward to sleeping in their new log house.

CHAPTER 14

Winter and a Big Surprise

Winter came early in the fall of 1921.The snow came in the middle of October and stayed. The weather was not too cold and the days were quite sunny between storms.

John had been to Pathlow right after the harvest and moving into the new house. He had bought a small shotgun and a 30-30 rifle. He thought that he may be able to get a few Partridge and Prairie Chickens with the shotgun and maybe a deer or two with the rifle. He had tried to shoot the birds with the 22 but you had to be a real good shot to get any. The shotgun would give him a better chance.

Florence was kept busy with the house and the baby. She still looked after the chickens and all the stock if John was away. They had got good returns from their garden and she had put up many jars of preserves. John on the other hand had been hauling straw and hay and some grain for the animals. Most of it was in exchange for the work he had done helping the other farmers with the harvest. In this way it did not cost much to live so the pension cheque was going farther all the time. In a few weeks John would have to sell four of his seven pigs. They were males and he would keep the other male and butcher it for their own use. The two sows he would keep for breeding.

When Frank Smith had brought his stallion over to breed Queen he had told John that he would have to castrate the pigs before they were sold or butchered. The colt and calf could wait until next spring. John had told him he didn't know anything about how to do that so Frank had told him he would come around in the fall and give him a hand. Frank made extra money by taking his stallion around to the different farms and by doing some vet work for the farmers. Usually the pay was in meat or some other commodity, money did not change hands very often. In this way everyone was able to get what they needed done and did not have to spend money to get it. The only exception was the fee for the stallion, it had to be cash and was guaranteed for five dollars.

Frank was a little man and it looked funny when he would drive up with a small pony pulling a two wheel cart with Frank sitting on the seat leading a big stallion behind him. But the people were pleased to be able to get this kind of service and Frank would always show up when he was needed.

One morning when John was hauling some manure from the chicken pen to spread on the garden, he heard a team coming. He could hear the crunching of the sleigh in the snow and the rattle of the harness. It was quite a ways away but in the cool clear weather noise travelled a long way.

It wasn't long before Frank Smith and his wife Bertha drove up in a little one seater cutter. It was a good thing that Frank was small because his wife took up at least three quarters of the seat. John waved to them and by the time he got to the house Bertha had already gone inside and Frank was turning the team around and going to the barn. He hollered at John, "Come on lets get to work on your pigs."

John shouted back, "O.K. I will be right with you."

They unhooked both teams and put them in the barn, there was always an extra in the daytime as the cows and other horses were out in the fenced area behind the barn. The straw was piled there and the fence ran down to the well so they could be watered in the morning and at night without having to lead them down to the well.

Frank went back to his cutter and got out a little box and brought it over to the pig pen. He told John that they would have to catch one pig at a time and John would have to hold the pig down on its back while he did his work. He said that John would have to hang on tight as a pig was strong and if they got away they would have a hell of a job catching them again.

The men chased the male pigs into a small corral by the barn and they started their work. John got the first pig held down and Frank opened up his little box and took out a very sharp looking knife and a bottle of Creoline. He then slit the pig open, cut off the testes and poured on some of the Creoline. The pig screeched so loud that John thought it was going to deafen him. All that Frank said was "let that one go and grab another one John before they all get spooked."

When they had finished with the five pigs John was in a real sweat. Not so much from holding the pigs but from the way thing were done and the noise that the pigs made. It did not seem to bother Frank at all but he had been doing this for some time and it was just another job to him. John was thinking about the spring and King the colt and Lightning the bull. He did not think he was going to relish doing them. Another thing it was dinner time and he did not feel too much like eating right now. John said as much to Frank and the reply was not what he expected.

Frank just grinned and said. "It used to bother me to but then I just think better them than me and it doesn't bother me any more."

He also told John to watch the pigs for a few days to make sure that there was no infection. If there was he should put on some more Creoline and if it got no better to get in touch with him. He also said it would be a good idea if he kept them away from the other pigs for a few days until they had healed.

With this the men went up for dinner and had a good talk about just about everything from the latest news and of course farming. After the Smiths had gone Florence turned to John and said.

"My God what were you doing to those poor animals out there we could hear them in the house. Did you have to hurt them that much?"

When John started to tell her what they had done she cut him off and said she didn't want to hear any more. With that John went back to work glad that he did not have to tell her any more.

Everything went fine for the next few days an John was busy cutting wood at a clearing behind the barn. He needed more room for the stock corral and the small trees would be good for fire wood and the bigger ones for lumber. He needed to build some good barns, chicken coops and pig pens. He could not use the straw barns after the winter as the roof would leak and get heavy when wet. He was sitting on a stump having a smoke when he heard a horse coming and someone whistling.

When John looked down toward the house he saw a man on a horse coming up the road and Christ it was Jimmy. God John thought I'm in trouble now after me selling him that shotgun that blew him right out of his buggy. He thought for a minute and then decided he had better face the music so he waved to Jimmy and shouted that he was over behind the barn. Then John thought that bloody half breed may just shoot my head right off!

When Jimmy got close to where John was he noticed a big sack full of something over his horses back behind the saddle. Jimmy was grinning when he came up. Then he said to John.

"Here is the deer I promised you for that cannon you sold me for a shotgun. I bet you never expected to see me unless it was to fill you full of lead. But a deal is a deal and anyway I traded that shotgun to a cousin of mine for two good dogs. We never got along too well and I hope that gun knocks the shoulder right off the bastard."

John sat for a minute and could hardly believe his ears. Then he jumped up and went over and shook Jimmy's hand and said, "Thanks Jimmy, I am glad there is no hard feelings. I thought afterwards that was a dirty trick to play on you but I knew you were a good hunter and maybe would know how to handle that gun".

Both men burst out laughing and finally Jimmy said. "I bet that gun had been fired no more than once by anyone. I'll also bet that it will travel many miles before those two boxes of shells are used up, unless some one breaks it over a tree after they have been set on their ass."

Both men burst out laughing again and then Jimmy asked where they could put the deer. It was cut up in Quarters and could be hung up easy. There would be no worry about it spoiling as it would stay frozen as long as it was outside and out of the sun.

John said he had a small grain building by the barn and it was not to full so maybe they could hang it in there.

The two men carried the meat into the shed and hung it up. Then they went up to the house to have tea and a sandwich. After they had finished Jimmy went on his way but not before telling John. "Next time we do a trade I will try whatever it is out first even if it does wake up the baby." The men had another good laugh and then said good bye.

When November the eleventh came around Bart and John went to Pathlow for Armistice Day only this year they travelled by caboose because of the early winter. They had a lot of time to talk on the way there and back. It was nice and warm in the caboose and they even left the war alone long enough to make some plans.

John had shipped all his male pigs but the one he was going to butcher. He told Bart that he was going to butcher a pig but didn't know that much about what he had to do.

Bart answered with, "I am going to butcher a steer so I will come up and help you with your pig and you can help me with the steer. When we get finished we can trade some of the meat and then we won't have to eat the same thing all the time. That also will save me killing a pig."

John agreed that would be a good idea but he owed Frank smith some of the pig for some work he had done for him.

Bart grinned and said, "That works out better still, when you take your meat over to Frank's stop by our place and I will give you the beef I owe him. It will only be a couple of miles out of your way and you can drop off Florence for a visit while you are gone. The women can then plan Christmas and New Years."

The men agreed on a day and were both happy with their plans. John also told Bart about getting the deer from Jimmy.

Bart laughed and said to John. "That is the best thing that I have ever heard. I will have to stop in and see Walter on the way home just so I can rub it in about you getting the deer. Remember he said you would never get paid. I like to give old Walter a jab whenever I get the chance."

Everything went well with the butchering and the visits over the Christmas and New Years also went very well. It was a very cold winter and when John and Florence got home from the Fords New Years night they really knew it had been cold. When they went into the house the fire had burnt out and it was as cold as outside. When they had lit the coal oil lamp and set it on the table they saw what was left of a pitcher of milk that had been left when they went out in a hurry. The glass was laying on both sides broken in half and a chunk of ice milk the shape of the pitcher sat there like it had been a sculpture.

Florence looked at John and said. "Don't tell me it isn't cold out side. I think I will go out to the barn while you put the horses away and this place warms up a bit.

John said, "Better than that the caboose is warm, I will unhook the team right here in front of the house and you and Helen can wait in there until the house gets warm."

They both agreed that this was a good idea and even Helen did not protest to the warm caboose.

Everything was pretty normal for the rest of the winter except that it was so cold that they burned more wood than they expected they would. This meant that John had to cut up some old dry trees to make up the difference.

They had the wood cutting bee as usual and John got some more lumber cut before the spring breakup. It was a tough winter but they had made some more headway with the homestead. Their stock was to increase in the spring and this would only add to the assets of the of the homestead. They were now looking forward to spring and some nice warm weather.

CHAPTER 15

Spring with Good and Bad Luck

After the cold winter spring started to come early. The roads broke up and the mud would be a mess in the daytime and frozen at night. There wasn't much that could be done at this time of year. John had hauled all the manure out and spread it on the garden when he cleaned the barns in the winter. The rest was piled back at the edge of the clearing. It could be used later and would rot to be even better when spread.

John spent most of his time starting to build a barn from the lumber he had cut. He would still put straw around the sides in the winter but the roof would shed the rain better than a straw roof. A chicken coop would be at one end with a shed between to store grain. This would make it easy to feed the stock. The pig pen was at the other side of the barn with its own fenced in area. The fence was made of poles but were closer together than the corral that was behind the barn for the cows and horses.

John enjoyed building and even Florence would come out and help drive nails when she could. Helen would be in a box nearby and would babble away as if she was the foreman of the job. This made

Florence say.

"I bet if she wasn't in that box Helen would be over here telling us what to do. That box was a good idea, it keeps her out of the mud and out of our way."

"Yes", John said, "she sure is a chatter box, just think she will be a year old soon. Just think what it will be like next year at this time."

Florence nodded in agreement and replied, "I don't want to even think about that. It wasn't too bad last year picking berries but I don't know what I will do this year she will be off all over the place. With bush all around it would be easy for her to get lost."

John agreed saying, "Maybe you will have to tie her to you with a rope so you can keep track of her."

"Golly John", Florence answered, "she is not one of your stock you know. She is a little girl but I guess we will have to think of some way to keep track of her."

John got a bright look on his face and said, "You know I hear that a dog will stay close to children and look after them. Alex has a nice old mutt over at his place he wants to give away. He is only about a year old and would be good company for you when I am not around. He is part sheep dog so he should be gentle."

"That might be a good idea," Florence agreed, "it does get some lonely here when one is by oneself."

It didn't take much more than that to be said for the next day John went over to Alex's place and came home with a cute dog. When they walked up to the house the dog was following behind him. When John opened the door the dog waited until he was asked to come inside. Florence took one look at he dog and seemed to like him. "What is his name" she asked.

"Jip", John answered, "cute little bugger isn't he!"

"Yes he is, but save your barn yard talk for out there' Florence retorted, "Helen will learn that kind of talk soon enough."

John shrugged his shoulders and said, "Well look at that, he has gone over to where Helen is playing and laid down beside her. I guess you now have your watch dog for when you are picking berries."

They both laughed and looked pleased at what the dog had done.

Spring went along just fine. The trees were starting to bud and some of the grass was starting to show green. It was a nice time of the year after a cold winter.

John had ploughed the garden and was just about ready for planting. Florence was getting all the seeds ready and was getting her canning equipment ready for the strawberry season. When the sun got hot and the days long it did not take very long for the berries to come.

The stock were doing well. Bossy had freshened and now had a little heifer which they called Betty. Queen had foaled and she had a little filly which was called Lizzy. The sow had eleven pigs but two died within a day or so. Even at that the stock was growing and the homestead was starting to look like a farm. If John could get more land cleared and broken for growing grain maybe they might even make a little money.

One Saturday night when John had finished with the team he let the horses out of the corral to forage for themselves along the clearing. There was some nice fresh peavine coming up and they would enjoy the fresh feed after a winter of hay and straw. The garden had a high fence around it to keep out the deer so there would be no problem there. It would save looking after them for a day because there was water in the stream and he was not going to use them the next day. They would not stray far away from the barn. He would be busy the next day fixing harness and anything else that needed repaired around the place. On Sunday afternoon John had seen Queen and the two colts at the back of the clearing, but he could not see Shortly or Claire. He would have to go find them after supper because he wanted to go to town tomorrow and get some seed potatoes and other seeds that they needed for the garden.

After supper was over John told Florence he was going to go look for the two horses that he had not seen all day. She just nodded and he was on his way.

John walked all around the clearing to see if he could see a trail that the horses might have taken. It had not rained for a few days so the ground was hard and not easy to read any signs. He kept going in ever increasing circles until dark but found no sigh of either horse. He headed back to the barn for he still had the other stock to feed and the cows to milk.

The next morning John was up at the crack of dawn and went out to the barn to look and see if the horses had come back. He could not see them anywhere so he went back and had breakfast. He told Florence as soon as he had finished the chores he would go back out and look for the two horses. Maybe she should make him a bite to eat so if he got too far away he would not have to come back for dinner. He told her that if the horses weren't moving they could be standing still behind some trees and be very hard to find. He could not understand why they had not come back the night before. It was not like them to not come in for their oats.

When John left he took a halter with him for he knew he could walk up to Shorty anyplace. Now Claire had a mind of his own and was more spirited but if he led Shorty home Claire would follow along.

John walked through the bush and followed trails most of the morning. He started down toward the creek to have a drink and his sandwiches. When he went under some tall willow trees the ground was still damp and he noticed some tracks. They were going down to the creek also. He had never been this far along before and he did not know what to expect. When he was getting close to where the creek should be he heard a horse whinny so he picked up his pace along the narrow trail. It must be a deer trail because no stock had ever been run in here.

John came over a little knoll and could see Shorty standing looking into a grassy spot. The horse turned his head toward John and whinnied again. John hurried down to where Shorty was and then he notice Claire was in the middle of the grassy spot and just his head and part of his neck was sticking out of the mud.

My God John thought quicksand what the Hell am I going to do now. He spoke to Claire and the horse just rolled his eyes and tried to move a little but he could not seem to move. John looked the situation over and started to make some plans.

The trouble was if he took Shorty away Claire would get all excited and try to move some more and only make matters worse. He would have to hurry as it looked like the horse was starting to shiver now. He was half thinking and half talking out loud to himself. He then hit on the idea of tying Shorty to a tree with the halter, in that way he would not venture into the quicksand. but would be company for Claire. John did this then set off back to the homestead to get what he needed to pull Claire out of the quicksand.

When John arrived back at the house he told Florence what had happened. She asked him if he had anything to eat yet. She could see the lunch she had given him still in his jacket pocket. He told her no there was no time for that he would eat on the way back. He had been so worked up that food was the last thing on his mind.

John decided that he would put a harness on Queen and some heavy rope with the log chain and take her back to the site. He could then use Shorty to pull Claire out of the Quicksand. He would have to lock the colts in the barn or they would follow and get into trouble also. When he talked this over with Florence she said.

"If what you say is true maybe we had better take some blankets along to cover Claire when you get him out. I will make up some more food for you for God knows when you will get back. I will bring Queen back so the colt can feed and if you are to late I will have to do the chores anyway. That sounded good to John and they also were going to take the dog along as he would help Florence find her way back as the trail was not that good.

John picked up some more tobacco and his pouch and as he passed the wood pile he picked up the axe. They harnessed the horse put the blankets on her back and set out along the trail to help Claire out of the Quicksand. Queen did not want to leave her colt but after a while she followed without too much fuss.

When they got down to the creek John put the harness on Shorty and hooked the log chain to a single tree. At the end of the chain he had a short length of heavy rope. As he was going out to put it around Claire's neck Florence shouted at him. "Don't go out there without something on the mud or we will have to pull you out also".

"God your right", John gasped, "I was so excited about getting Claire out that I didn't even think about that."

John took the axe and cut some willow branches and small limbs. He then piled them on the mud in front of Claire. Then he put the rope around the horses neck and came back to Shorty. Florence gave him the rope from the halter and John started to ease Shorty ahead to tighten up the rope. When the rope was tight he talked softly to both horse's. Shorty had been used to pulling stumps so he just put his weight against the collar and leaned into the pull. Claire was quite weak and was not much help. Shorty was pulling very hard and John thought he might break the neck of Claire. He was just about to give up when Claire started to move and came out of the Quicksand very slowly. When he got to solid land he just fell on the ground and did not move.

John untied the rope around his neck and Florence lead Shorty away and tied him to a tree beside Queen. John took some soft branches and brushed as much mud off Claire as he could. He then put the blankets over Claire. The horse was starting to shiver quite a lot.

Florence said she would take Queen back and that he had better keep Shorty there just for company for Claire. John said O.K. and that she had better start back now before too late. He also told her not to worry if he was here all night as he would build a fire and stay until Claire was able to walk home. If he was still there in the morning would she bring him something to eat. He was fine for the night as he had extra food and lots of tobacco.

After Florence had left John started a fire close to Claire. He noticed that the horse was now coughing every once in a while. He went and picked some grass but Claire would not eat any. He moved Shorty to where there was some grass but left him tied on a long rope. He did not want another horse in the Quicksand.

Darkness came and there was still no change except that Claire coughed more often. He was still shivering and his eyes were fogged over. John did not feel much like eating anything but thought he had better because it looked like he would be here for the rest of the night. He finished his lunch and went down to the creek to get a drink. He picked up some more wood on the way back and settled in for the night.

John must have gone to sleep because the next thing he knew it was getting light. The fire had burned down and the air was cool. He looked over at Claire but could see no movement. He looked at the side of the horse and could not see them moving. When John walked over to touch the horse he felt cold. He then just stood there looking at the horse he had been so proud to own. a few tears rolled down his cheeks. He shook his head to clear the mist from his eyes and walked over to Shorty and said. "Well old boy you have lost your friend. Let's go home and get a shovel and come back and cover him with dirt. I don't want some wild animals eating my horse."

John rolled a smoke and took a couple of deep drags, then with one more look at Claire he untied Shorty and with his head hanging low headed for home.

When John got home Florence came down to the barn to see him. She could tell that all was not right. When John told her what had happened she shed a tear or two for poor old Claire. John told her that after he had something to eat he would go back and bury Claire. He would also take some wire fencing with him and put the wire around the Quicksand. They could not afford to lose any more stock.

It took them a while to get over the loss of one of their first horses. It wasn't as easy to use Queen with Shorty and the colt had to be along all the time. They would have to make things do until they could buy another horse to work with Shorty.

Spring had been good and bad. They had gained some stock but they had lost a real good horse. It would be a long time before either Florence or John would forget the spring of 1922.

CHAPTER 16

Hot Dry Summer and Cold Fall

After John and Florence got over the loss of Claire they got back to work as usual. The summer started very hot and there did not seem to be a let up in sight.

John would have some more road work in July but with only shorty left of his team he didn't know just what to do Queen was a willing worker but it wasn't too good with the colt around all the time.

One day on the way back from town John had stopped in to see how Alex was making out. He told him about the loss of his horse and how it was going to be a problem with a colt along. Alex said that he had a solution to his problem and proceeded to tell John. "Why don't you take that big horse of mine, Jock. He is about the same size as your horse."

"I can't do that", John replied, "you will need him to go to town with."

"Oh no,", Alex retorted, "I have another horse now that is smaller and I use it to go to town with. I just use the small buggy in the summer so one horse is all I need. Anyway if you have Jock I won't have to feed him. When winter comes and I have to use the caboose you will be finished with him. See what a good deal it is for both of us."

"Hell yes it sure is good deal for me anyway. Then I won't have to buy another horse until fall when they are a little cheaper."

John thanked Alex for the kind offer and set off for home with Jock tied behind. When he drove into the yard Florence met him at the door and said.

"Where the heck did you get enough money to buy another horse? Did you strike it rich or something?"

John grinned and replied, "This is Alex's horse and he has lent him to me for the summer. He will make a good mate for Shorty and I will be able to do road work without the bother of the colt being in the way all the time."

"Sounds like you made a good deal there," Florence answered, "did you find out in town where the road work is going to be this year?"

"Yes," John replied, "when I was in the Municipal Office they told me that it will be along Lake Lenore just South of St. Brieux. That won't be as far away as the last years. Maybe I can get to know some of the French people that live there. They are good farmers and maybe they will have a horse to sell me in the fall. They also have the rights to fish White Fish in Lake Lenore so maybe we can get some from them this winter. It sure would help change the diet a little bit. Anyway I miss the fish that we used to get all the time back home in Nova Scotia."

"By golly that would be nice for a change." Florence interjected, "It sure would be nice to have a good fish chowder once in a while. Don't wait until next fall. Bring some home on the weekends with you if you can."

"I sure will try" John said, "but I won't be going for a week or so and I have to go back and cut some hay before it all dries out. They say it has been so dry this year that even some of the swamps have dried out, so I had better get up in the hills and get hay cut for next winter."

While John was cutting hay and hauling it home, Florence was out again picking berries. With the warm dry weather they were a little harder to find than in years before. She had to go further away from home and stay close to the creeks. There was no water in the creeks now but it had stayed wet there longer in the spring so the berries were best there.

Florence was sure glad that she had the dog Jip along not only to help keep track of Helen but she had also heard that bears sometimes like to pick berries. Most of the bears were up north farther but sometimes they would wander down around the farms.

Not only the berry picking and canning kept Florence busy but with John away all week she had to look after all the animals. They were getting to have quite a few pigs now and she never did like looking after them. They were so dirty and stunk to high heaven. Milking the cows was not her favorite job either. When it came right down to it she didn't really like the homestead that much. Maybe it was because the work was so hard, she had not been used to this type of work and with John being gone so much it made for a lonely life. She had been living in Boston before they had got married and this was a far cry from the big city. But what the heck she had made her move and she had better make the best of it. They were eating pretty good and had a daughter to look after. Just the same sometimes when she was by herself she would day dream about Boston and even Nova Scotia.

The weather kept on very hot and there had been no rain. Not even a thunder storm to cool it down once in a while. The crops that had been put in had started well but now they were showing signs that the crop would not be too good. For some of the farmers the harvest would be very poor this year unless it rained soon.

One Saturday John came home early from working on the road.

They had finished one part and would be moving to another section on Monday morning. When he got near Florence could tell he was all excited. He had jumped off the wagon and was hurrying to the house. In his hand he was carrying a wet sack and showed her what was inside.

"You brought some fish". Florence exclaimed, "Will they be O.K. in this hot weather?"

"Oh sure," John replied, "I had a bucket of water and kept the sack wet all the way home. Anyway they had just been caught and are real fresh. Could you make some fish chowder for supper?"

"Sure thing", Florence answered, "It may be a little late but it sure will be nice to have some fresh fish. You can tell me all about it later while we are eating."

Later when they were enjoying their supper John told Florence all about his week working south of St. Brieux.

He began with , "Did you know that the French people that live around St. Brieux have all come over straight from France? They were given a good deal on the land and the rights to the fish in Lake Lenore if they would settle there. I always thought they had come from Quebec and when I mentioned that they soon set me straight. The soil by the lake in not that good so they did not pay a lot for it. They all have cattle, pigs and real nice horses. Some of their horses are wild ones that they had gone South and caught for themselves. They are not real big horses but they sure are fast and strong. Also they are not as hard to look after as they are used to looking after themselves."

"You sound like you like these people very much." Florence finally was able to say. "did you have any trouble talking to them?"

"Not at all, most of them speak good English." John replied, "And I even tried a few words that I had learned while I was in France during the war. Some of the ones I didn't try but I heard them being used on the road gang when some of their horses wouldn't behave.

It's funny the bad words seem to be the ones you learn first."

Florence was impressed with what John had told her. These people only lived a short distance away. St. Brieux was only about ten miles but that was the way of homesteading. People were too busy working all the time to get around the country very often. Finally Florence said to John.

"I guess they have a big Catholic church there. You can always tell who has settled around a town by the church that is there. It is just like little districts from another land."

"Yes", John replied, "it sure makes it interesting when you go to these places. I hope we can go together sometime. You don't get much chance to get anywhere. You must be lonely here when I am away."

"It sure is lonely all right," Florence sighed and said, "But you leave me enough work to do that I don't really get a chance to let it bother me too much. I worry though what would happen if Helen or I got sick and we were here by ourselves."

"I think about that to." was John's reply, "I will be glad when we get some land broken and I can stay home and farm. But in the meantime I have to earn money any way I can."

It was late now and they had both enjoyed the fish for supper. Both had work to do before it got too late so no more was said about the lonely life."

When John had finished working on the road and was to go out looking for work with the harvest he told Florence that it might be hard this year to find much work as it had been so dry that most of the farmers could look after it themselves.

Florence looked sad and said to John. "This will make it tough on us this winter. You will need the grain and straw for the stock and the extra money would be handy. Maybe we had better not buy another horse this fall. That would give us one less mouth to feed."

John thought for a while then replied, "That makes good sense.

I can still use Jock for a while longer and for hauling wood and any other work

Shorty and Queen will do just fine. It is a good job that I got some hay cut this summer. The straw that I do pick up will not be very good this year."

It was decided then that they would get rid of as many pigs that they could. They would butcher as soon as it was cold enough to keep the meat. John said that they would be able to trade some of their meat for fish. He had been told this by some of the people he had worked with on the road.

The harvest was very poor and the grain very short because of the dry weather. John got some work in but not as much as the years before. He had managed to get a good supply of straw from some of the farmers who had also got rid of a lot of their stock. The straw wasn't that good but was better than nothing.

Just after the first of October the weather got real cold. The ground was frozen most of the time so all work stopped in the fields. By Thanksgiving the second Monday of the month there was snow on the ground and more was falling every day. If this kept up it would be a hard long winter.

John and Florence were concerned about the turn of events yet they could do nothing about the weather. They sometimes spent a lot of time talking about ways they could make some extra money At least they had lots of meat and eggs. They made their own butter and bought wheat and had it ground for cereal. They really had to buy very little to get along. But it would be nice to be able to gain some headway into getting a working farm.

John had said, "With all the trees on their homestead they would never be without fire wood"

And Florence answered with, "And if we don't eat up all our stock I guess we will survive. At least we did not have a crop to fail this year."

CHAPTER 17

A Winter Trapping Trip

The weather into November stayed very cold. When it did warm up it would only snow some more. The days were clear in the cold weather but were getting shorter. John was sure glad that Florence had thought to check the chinks between the logs on the house. she had plastered more mud where the old mud had fallen out. The house was nice and warm with the kitchen stove and the heater going. The new barn and pens were not as warm as the old straw ones. John had piled as much straw as he could against the outside walls to help keep out he wind. As long as the barn was full it wasn't too bad.

The ice in the watering trough had to be chopped out every two or three days. Just doing the chores and keeping lots of wood at the house was a full time job.

All the stock had been fixed by Frank Smith and John was glad that was over. Now if he could just find some other way to get a little extra money everything would be alright.

Bart and John went on the usual November the eleventh trip and the women had a good visit and planned for the Christmas and New Years get to together. With the cold weather there had not been much travelling done.

One day in December when John was working in the barn yard Jimmy came over to see him.

They talked for a while then Jimmy said. "John I hear you would like to earn some extra money as you did not get that much work at harvest time. I am going up to Candle Lake in early January to do some trapping. If you want to come along as a partner you are welcome."

John thought for a minute then replied, "I don't know anything about trapping. How could I of any help to you?"

Jimmy didn't hesitate in his reply, "You could bring along a second dog team, also someone has to look after the furs and do the cooking. You could also trap some smaller animals close to where we will be staying. There is a cabin that I can use up there. What do you think?"

"Let's go up to the house and see what Florence thinks about the idea." John said as he lead Jimmy's horse into the barn and he added. "It's too bloody cold out here to stand around talking. Anyway we can have a cup of something hot to drink".

The men walked into the house after brushing the snow from their feet. The house was nice and warm and Florence had already had the tea on as she knew they would be in for a cup.

The men sat at the table and asked Florence to join them as they wanted her to hear about their plan to go trapping.

Jimmy explained that he would look after getting a dog team for John. He had two sleds so John could use one. He also said that he had a lot of friends and relatives between here and Candle lake. Some of them also trapped in that area. They would stop over at their places on the way up and any other nights they could sleep in a tent.

They talked for some time about this. The biggest worry that Florence had was being alone and looking after all the stock. Also what if she or Helen got sick what would she do?

More talk took place but in the long run they decided to go ahead with the trapping trip. They would leave right after New Years.

Florence and John had Christmas at the Fords and they came back for New Years. They had a good time and many stories went the round. The children were getting old enough to play together which helped them to entertain themselves.

There was a lot of talk about John and his trapping expedition. They all hoped it would work out well. The Fords offered to take Florence and the stock to their place but Florence refused saying she could look after herself. Bart said that John should make sure the neighbour checked in once in a while to make sure everything was all right.

A couple of days after New Years John said goodbye to Florence and Helen and was on his way to Candle Lake with Jimmy. He had piled a lot of wood up close to the house and had put hay and straw as close to the barn as he could. The hardest job for Florence would be watering the stock. she would have to keep chopping out the watering trough. Also she had Helen to look after when she was working outside.

John was thinking of these things as he headed out to Jimmy's place. It was not even light yet but he wanted to be there so they could have a early start. It would take a couple of hours to walk there and it would be light by that time.

When John got to Jimmy's place he was already hooking up the dog teams. He had the two sleighs loaded and was about ready to go. He saw John and waved. "we are about ready to go you can take the back sled and just follow me. You will learn as we go how to handle the dogs. Most of them are well trained and I have been out with them in the last few days. So let's get going and trap some furs."

With this Jimmy hollered at his team and they were off down the road heading for Kinistino. Johns team jumped into their harness and just about left him behind. He would have a lot to learn and that was the first thing. Be ready to move when the dogs were.

The travel along the road was much different than with horses. The dogs made good time and John spent some time riding on the back of the sleigh and some time running behind to keep warm. Every once in a while Jimmy would slow the dogs down to give them a bit of a rest. He did not want to wear them out the first day. They would be stopping at Kinistino tonight so that would not be too long of a trip. He had a brother living there so they would stay at his place for the night. The next day they would try to get to Birch Hills where he had another relative they could stay with for the night.

At noon they stopped at a small bluff of trees for dinner. They had some frozen sandwiches and Jimmy had built a small fire and made tea. He told John that a good cup of tea would make up for the frozen sandwiches any time.

They arrived in Kinistino just at dark and started to put the dogs up for the night. Jimmy showed John how to feed the dogs. He had brought some frozen deer meat with him on the sleigh. The dogs were to be fed only in the morning and at night. The biggest meal would be at night then they would not have to run on too full a stomach. Also he pointed out that they could not be tied too close together or they would fight over the food.

The next morning they were off again bright and early. It was still dark when they left. Jimmy wanted to get to Birch Hills early and the next day they would try to reach Prince Albert. That would be a long run and if they got in early tonight then the dogs would have a good rest.

Everything went fine and they arrived early in Birch Hills. John was getting on to running a dog team and Jimmy let him take the lead a few times. He also let John look after the teams so he was learning everything he could. This gave him some time to himself and he would think of home and wonder it everything was O.K. with Florence and Helen.

The next morning they left two hours before light. It would be a long haul into Prince Albert. They would buy the rest of their supplies there. They would have to get the permits and enough supplies to last them till they came out.

They stopped at Prince Albert at a small house on the outskirts. It was well after dark and it was not easy for John to look after the dogs. This was another of Jimmy's relatives and this made John think, how many relative and friends does this half breed have? It seems that he has them all over the country. But I'm sure as hell not going to grumble if it keeps us from sleeping in a tent in the middle of winter.

After John had finished with the dogs he went into the house to have something to eat. When he was finished they sat by the fire and had a smoke. After being in the cold all day and now sitting in the warm room the next thing John knew he had fallen asleep in the chair. He woke with a start to hear everyone laughing. Then he heard Jimmy say.

"I don't know if I have a good partner or not he keeps going to sleep on me. But he had better enjoy the heat for the next couple of nights we may have to sleep in the tent.

Everyone even John had a good laugh at this. He wasn't looking forward to sleeping in the tent and was going to enjoy the heat as long as he could.

The next morning they picked up what they needed and were on the road as soon as could be. After they had been out of town a few miles past the North Saskatchewan river the road became just a trail. The snow wasn't deep and the dogs followed the trail without much trouble. The trees were small pine and looked pretty with the green showing out from a capping of snow. Most of the trees were small but there were a few good sized ones.

That night they camped in the trees with the tent. There was no wind and John was surprised how warm it was in the tent. Jimmy knew just what to do and all in all the night was not too bad. They spent a couple of more nights sleeping out then arrived at the cabin about noon on the fourth day. It was just a small place but looked like a big Hotel to John. There were a couple of bunks inside, a good stove and some home made furniture. There was some wood in the lean-to but John would have to cut some dry wood to keep them going. This would be their home for the next while so they might just as well make it as comfortable as they could. Jimmy was going out the next day to see if he could get some meat for them to use while they were here. They had not brought much with them so John hoped he would be lucky.

The next day Jimmy was not gone very long when he came back with an nice Moose. He said that this would keep them in meat for some time and feed the dogs. They lifted the quarters of meat up off the ground so that the animals would not get into it. It was a good thing they had a good saw because when the meat was frozen it sure was hard to cut.

When they had been there a couple of days a visitor showed up at the cabin. John was there alone so he asked the man in for dinner. He explained that his partner would be back later in the afternoon as he was out setting some traps.

The man said that was fine, then he told John that he was a Government person and that he looked after this area to keep track of the trappers and to make sure they all had the proper papers.

John told him that Jimmy was looking after that sort of stuff. He asked the man if he wanted to stay the night and he said he would. He had food for his own dog team and would just make his bed up on the floor.

That night John made a real good moose stew. The man said it was real good and this pleased John. Jimmy didn't look too pleased and this made John wonder why. The man had checked all the papers and seemed happy.

The next morning when the man was ready to leave he turned to

John and said. "I might just come back for some more of that good moose stew. Don't you start up a restaurant and sell any of that good food." With that he winked at John and was on his way.

"What the hell was that all about?' John asked Jimmy.

"He was just letting us know that we shot a moose out of season and as long as we just used it for food he will not say anything. They are a good bunch of guys as long as you don't go too far. They know that we have to live also."

Time went by fast over the next while. The weather stayed cold but the cabin was nice and warm. It kept John busy chopping wood and he had to get dry trees and they were hard to find close by. With the few furs that they got he was kept busy looking after the dogs and keeping them in food.He had shot a few birds close to the cabin and this had given them a little change in diet. He often thought of home when he was by himself. He spent a lot of time alone while Jimmy was out trapping. They were not doing too well and Jimmy said they had come too late. Also the area was getting trapped out.

One day in early March Jimmy said they should get ready to head for home. Even though they did not have many furs he could feel a warm spell coming and they did not want to get caught in the bush and the snow gone. John did not argue with this as he had seen Jimmy forecast the weather right too many times.

Within two days they were loaded and leaving the cabin. The weather was already mild and it was raining. There had not been that much snow fall this winter it had been mostly clear and cold. They had better hurry or the snow would be gone.

The first day wasn't too bad, but by the second day the snow was disappearing quite fast . Sometimes they would hit parts of the trail where there were bare spots. The dogs were getting very tired and the load was very hard to pull. They even dumped off a few thing that they could do without. But still the dogs were having a tough time.

Just before they reached the North Saskatchewan river two of the dogs collapsed and had to be shot. The river was still frozen over so they crossed into Prince Albert. The weather was still very warm and most of the snow was gone. There were remarks all over about how early spring had come, but look out it could get cold and snow again in no time.

The next day John and Jimmy left the relative's place and went down town and sold everything except their guns and Jimmy's traps. They then caught the train to Melfort and would stay there over night. The next morning they would get the train to Ethelton and then walk home from there.

When John and Jimmy got off the train at Ethelton they picked up the mail and then started walking home. It was starting to get cold again and was snowing a little bit. After they had walked about four miles Jimmy and John said goodbye and headed for their respective homes. John would be glad to see his family and to have a good home cooked meal made by Florence. He had no way of letting her know he was coming home and hoped that everything was fine.

It was just past noon when John walked into the yard at the homestead. Jip the dog came out to meet him and was jumping around in a circle and barking his head off. Florence came out to meet John also and Helen was right behind her. It was quite a homecoming and everyone was talking at once. With the dog barking and Helen trying to be heard it was some confusion. When they got to the house things got a little better.

Florence got something for John to eat and they had a better chance to talk. She had done very well and had not had any bad things happen. She said she would not stay alone again for that long of time in the winter time. Without even a phone it was taking too big a chance. John agreed and said he would not be going on another trapping trip for some time. When everything had been paid for they had only made about fifty dollars each. That wasn't very good money for all the work and hardships they had gone through.

Florence just shook her head and said, "We could have made that kind of money cutting wood and selling it in town. At least we would have got some of our land cleared at the same time.

They had been so busy talking about the winter that they hadn't noticed that the afternoon was nearly gone and it was getting dark outside. John went to the door and said "Man it is getting cold out there. The thermometer is already down to twenty below. Just what we need a cold spell and no snow left on the ground. Why couldn't it have stayed cold so we would not have had all that trouble getting home from up north.

"Yes", Florence replied, This is sure one tough part of the world. It can be nice and warm at forty above in the morning and thirty below by night time. Anyway get your chores done early as we still have a lot to talk about."

When John had finished supper and the chores, he and Florence sat and talked. He was very pleased at how she had looked after the stock and the homestead. But they both agreed that there would be no more money making trips without a lot of thought going into them first.

CHAPTER 18

Double Trouble Spring of 1923

There was cold and snow until about the middle of April. Then things really started to move. The weather got really warm and trees started to bud and a few birds started to show up from wintering in the south. The swallows were the first to be noticed. They would nest around the barn so they were the first seen in the spring.

John had been over to see Alex and had made the same deal as the year before. He was to use his horse Jock for the summer. He could not use Queen as she was close to foal time. He would have to start plowing the garden soon and would need two good horses. He sure hoped that he could buy another work horse soon. It would be another year or so before King would be big enough to work. He was a smaller horse than Shorty so he should still have another good sized work horse.

They had another good litter of pigs so things were looking good in that area. The chickens would start to set soon so maybe they would do alright there also.

John was now plowing up the garden area and getting it ready to plant. The nights seemed to be frost free now. One night when he was finished he let all the horses out the back of the corral so they could feed on some of the new shoots that had started to grow. It would do them good to have some fresh feed. The cattle were also enjoying the new feed. Bossy was close to freshening and he would have to keep a eye on her. He didn't want her to wander off to have her calf.

The next morning when John had driven Gertie in the barn to milk he had not noticed Bossy around anywhere. He would have to go look for her after breakfast.

When John finished eating he told Florence that he would have to go and look for Bossy. He did not think that she would stray too far but he did not want her having her calf out in the bush some where.

Florence nodded and said. "If you need a hand I can help look also. She might be laying down close by some where."

John replied, "Don't worry just yet I haven't even started to look. She might be laying down close by some where."

Florence handed John a bag and said. "Here are a couple of bacon sandwiches for you just in case you are gone for a while. Where are you going to start looking?"

"I don't know" was John's answer, "I will just start in the bush behind the corral and work my way back and forth until I can find a track. I wished to hell I had put a bell on her then I would have a better chance of finding her. I never thought and only put a bell on the milk cow."

"Well as you said we won't worry too much because we are not sure she has gone away." Florence looked at John and finished with. "Get going and find that cow so we can get back to the gardening."

John turned and set off to start the hunt for Bossy. He started at the back of the clearing behind the corral to look for tracks that were leading away from the barns. He went back and forth through the small shrubs but there were tracks all over from the horses and the cows He would have to go a little deeper into the trees to find a new track.

After about an hour of looking John still had not found a set of tracks. He sat down on a old fallen tree and rolled a smoke. He was mumbling to himself about where he would look next. It was not uncommon for a homesteader to mumble or talk to themselves when out alone some where. It was said that when they started answering themselves then they had been alone too long. He finished the smoke and ground it out with his heel. He then started down toward the creek. He could at least have a drink and start off again. He hoped to find a sign soon.

John followed the creek for a while. He was past the place where quicksand had been fenced off. There was no signs to be found here either. He thought to himself where the hell could have that cow got to anyway?

Every once in a while John would call out the name of the cow but there never was an answer of any kind. By noon he sat down under a tree and had his snack. The bacon would make him thirsty so he would have to head back toward the creek soon and get another drink.

John spent the rest of the afternoon checking all the game trails and along the creek and never found a sign. It was getting late and he started home. It would sure be nice if Bossy was there when he got back. But when he came up to the barn he did not see her any where.

That night when John was going to bed he said to Florence, "I will get up early in the morning and look for Bossy. I think I will take Jip with me. He might be of some help in finding that damn cow."

"Yes it sure is frustrating to know she is out there some place close by and you cannot find her." Florence continued with, "I will make you something to take along with you. If you are gone all day like you were to-day you will starve to death."

"Thanks" John replied, "I sure hope I won't be all day finding her."

John had finished the chores and his breakfast before first light. He called the dog and picked up a piece of rope then headed back for the bush to look for Bossy.

The sun was just shining on the tops of the trees and the tips looked silver with the new leaves just starting to come out. John looked at them and thought how pretty they looked. This might be a hard place but it still had its beauty in spite of everything else.

Jip and John walked though the bush and small clearings until noon. They were sitting under a tree for lunch. Jip was begging for food so John would throw a small piece of bread for him and he would chase it down the little game trail. Once when John threw a piece a good distance Jip didn't come back John got up to see what the dog was doing. He was standing beside a muddy spot and sniffing. John said to the dog. "What are you doing Jip."

When John walked up to where the dog was he could see a hoof print in the soft mud. He bent down to look and sure enough it was a cow's hoof print. John patted the dog on the head and said. "Good boy Jip, that is the first good sign we have had all day. Do you think you can follow it and find our cow."

John and Jip set off down the narrow game trail. Jip was in the lead and seemed to be sniffing along the trail. They had gone about a quarter of a mile when Jip stopped and put his head up in the air and then started back up the trail. John just stood there and wondered what the dog was doing now. He had only gone back about twenty feet when there was a low moo from the bush to the left.

John told the dog to stay and then started to look for a place where he could get through the thick trees and under brush to see where the noise had come from. He finally found a small opening and after about a half a dozen steps he was in a small clearing and there stood Bossy. He looked down in front of the cow were she was licking a small calf. He could tell at first glance that the calf was dead. And in his mind he wondered what to do next.

He petted Bossy on the head and said to her. "You poor cow we are going to have to get you home and away from your dead calf. But first I am going to milk you some. Your bag is so full it looks like it might break. It's a good job old Jip found you in time."

John did not realize that he had ben talking out loud but when he mentioned the dog's name Jip barked and Bossy got real excited. John spoke to her to try and settle her down. She had thought the dog would harm her calf. She did not seem to know that the calf was dead. Once John got her settled down he milked her some to relieve the pressure from her udder. He then put the rope around her neck and tried to lead her home.

There was no way that he cow would leave her calf and John was about to give up when Jip came up behind the cow and bit her on the leg. The cow just about jumped over top of John but he managed to get out of the way then jump in front of her to keep her going. They got onto the trail and started for home. She didn't like to leave her calf but Jip stayed behind her and kept her going. John thought he would have to come back tomorrow and bury the calf. The coyotes would likely have a good feed tonight. He hoped not he did not want them eating his calf.

After John had told Florence about the calf they both decided that they wanted the calf buried. Florence said she would do the chores and John could go back with a shovel and do the job right. It was light until late so he would have lots of time.

It took a few days for everyone to get over the still born calf. Jip was treated extra well because of his help in finding the cow. He was enjoying every bit of the special attention.

Everything was going along good until one morning when John went out to do the chores he heard a noise behind the barn in the corral. When he went outside he saw Queen had given birth to a foal. The colt was laying on the ground and the afterbirth was around it's neck. John hurried over to see what he could do. It was too late the colt had already choked and was dead. John thought what more can happen to my stock. This was just about too much to take.

After John had put Queen in the barn he had hauled the colt out to the manure pile behind the clearing. He covered over the colt and wondered if he would have to bury any thing else this spring. He went back to the barn and finished his chores.

When John got back to the house Florence asked him why he had been so long. Breakfast had been ready for a long time.

John looked at her for a while then said with a lump in his throat, "I just had to bury a colt and don't feel like much breakfast. What the Hell kind of luck is this we are having."

Florence put her arm around John's shoulder and said with a husky voice. "John maybe this is the end of our bad luck. You know they say bad luck always comes in threes. We have lost a horse, a calf and a colt. Let's hope that will be the end."

They both sat down and had a cup of coffee. What else could a person say at a time like this.

CHAPTER 19

A Better Last Half of 1923

The summer of 23 was hot but there was a few rain storms to help things grow. The Garden was really starting to show signs of being a good crop.

The stock were doing well also. After the loss of the colt and calf. The pigs had bred well and the pen was full of little ones. This would help when they could be sold The sows would be kept for future breeding.

There had been an auction sale at one of the homesteads just east of Pathlow. The owner had not been well so he decided to sell out and move back to Ontario where he had lived before. John thought he would go and see if he could buy some equipment or stock at a cheap price. So he hitched the team to the wagon early that morning and left for the auction.

When John got there some people were already looking over the stock and equipment. It wasn't long before the auctioneer started his chant and the people gathered around. The first things to be auctioned was the stock.

John was not looking for any cattle, pigs or chickens. He was more interested in the horses. He noticed one little mare that was about the same size as Alex's other horse. He thought if he could get a good buy on that one he could trade it to Alex for Jock. Then Alex would have two horses about the same size and he would have a good size Horse to work with Shorty. The price might not be too high as most farmers would be looking for bigger work horses. He hoped this would be the case.

When the bidding got around to the mare that John wanted no one seemed to be too interested. The auctioneer said "Let's have a bid on this nice little mare Flossie. She would be a good buggy horse for some one. She is very gentle so anyone could handle her."

John thought to himself. What the hell would Florence think if he brought a horse home with the name Flossie. Even worse if he traded her to Alex what would she think of him driving down the road and saying get up Flossie? He would have to worry about that later so he made a bid on the horse.

Finally a man beside John upped the bid and John countered with a little more. Things were quiet for a moment then the man beside John leaned over and said to John.

"Do you really want that little horse"?

John was so surprised that he could hardly answer but he finally said. "Why yes I need her to match another horse about the same size".

"Good" The other replied, "I was going to buy her for my son but he is a little too young yet, so you can have her. There is no need of us bidding against each other. I hope she works out for you."

John said, "Thanks that is very nice of you."

The man just grinned, nodded his head and walked away.

When John heard the auctioneer say sold he was so happy he could not keep the grin off his face. He had got a real good deal and he would worry about the name later.

As the day went on the things moved on to the equipment. John got a good buy on a seeder. It was not a big one but would be good enough for him because he would not be breaking a lot of land in the next while. He also was able to pick up some parts for the old mower and hay rake that he had. That would be a help because there was always something breaking on them. Now he would not have to go to town every time he needed a part.

When it came to the house hold things he was able to pick up a good cream separator and butter churn. Florence would be pleased for now she would not have to skim the cream off the top of the milk and shake it in a jar to make butter. In the summer time it was hard to get the milk cool enough to bring the cream to the top. It had to be put down in the well where it was cool and made for a lot of trips back and forth.

When John had got most everything he thought he could afford he settled up and started home. It looked quite funny with him in the wagon pulling a seeder behind with a horse tied to the seeder. One of the men remarked as he was going out of the yard "Jesus John you look like a freight train. Maybe you should go on the railroad tracks?"

Everyone who could hear this had a good laugh and John just waved and headed for home.

When John got home both Florence and Helen met him as he drove up to the house. Helen was all excited when she saw her dad and when she saw the horse she started to go toward it. Florence grabbed her and told her that this was a new horse and she didn't know if it liked little girls so she had better wait until they found out. Helen just looked at her mother and said. "But Shorty likes me."

Florence replied, "Yes but Shorty knows you and is used to you around. We don't know if this horse is quiet or not. Let's just wait for a while. Then she turned to John with, "What have we here it looks like you did a lot of buying today".

"Hey Florence", John said in a excited voice. "I did real good today. In the wagon here I have some mower and rake parts and the best is I got a real good buy on a cream separator and butter churn they even threw in the butter press. That should save you some work."

"That's real good," Florence said as she held on to Helen to keep her from going to the new horse. "It looks like you got some machinery and a horse to."

"I got the seeder cheap too as it is small and most farmers want the big ones. If I can get more trees cleared maybe I can break a few acres next summer and sow a crop the year after."

"That sounds good John but I thought you wanted a bigger work horse than that one behind the seeder. What are you going to do have a buggy horse just for going to town?"

"No no no," John answered, "I thought if I could trade her to Alex for Jock then he would have a matched team and we would have a matched team with Shorty and Jock".

"That's a good thought but do you think he will go for a deal like that?"

"Well maybe if you throw in a few loaves of bread, some home made butter and a jar or two of jam it would help cinch the deal." John then grinned and said, any way I can't keep a horse with a name like Flossie."

Florence's head shot up and she retorted. "You can't damn well trade one off with that name either. What do you think it would be like when Alex went into town and said whoa Flossie, get up Flossie, stand still Flossie."?

John was still grinning when he said, "Well as long as you weren't in the buggy with Alex I guess no one would really care too much."

With this they both had a good laugh even Helen laughed but she probably didn't know why.

A few days later when Florence had made up a few pounds of butter and baked some bread John put them in a sack and rode Queen over to Alex's place. He had Flossie [the horse] on a lead rope behind.

When he got to Alex's place he tied up the horses and went to the house. When he got to the door Alex yelled come in before he could even knock. Alex was sitting by the window smoking his pipe and reading one of his many western books that he enjoyed so much. He nodded for John to sit down and then said.

"Nice to see you neighbour. Sit down and we will have a beer. What have you got there in the sack?"

"Oh just a few loaves of bread, some fresh butter and a couple jars of jam."

"To hell with the beer John lets just have some of that stuff and cup of tea."

John said he was not hungry as he had just had a big breakfast. But he told Alex to go ahead and have something if he wanted to. He would just have a cup of tea and a smoke.

After Alex had made tea and was into about his fourth slice of bread covered thick in butter and jam, John got around to the reason he had come over.

John said to Alex. "I got this real nice little mare outside that would go real good with your other horse. They would make a nice team together as they are the same size. I thought maybe I could trade her to you for Jock then we would both have a matched team."

"Well", Alex replied, "I will have to have a look at this good deal that you say you have for me."

Alex hoisted himself out of the chair and both of the men went outside. Alex did not move too fast as he had difficulty with the size of his midriff. It was huge from where he had been cut open in the war. It was a lot of effort for him to look after his horses and a few chickens and a couple of pigs. He spent a lot of time reading so that the days would not be too long. He did not suffer for money as he rented his land for a share and he had a good pension cheque. It was a quiet life but that was the way he wanted it to be.

Alex looked the horse over and said to John. "That is a nice horse.

She would make up a nice team for me. But you would be getting much more of horse than I would. Do you think that would be right?"

The horse trading started and after a short while both men seemed pleased with the deal. Alex would make the trade if John would throw in another sack of goodies like he had brought over today, and five loads of logs that were good for fire wood. They shook hands on the deal. Alex went into the house and got John some Texas Ranger magazines to read and then told John to thank Florence for the wonderful food.

John said he would and then added "The name of the mare is Flossie and I would ask you not to call her by name if you are over at out place or if Florence is around."

Both men had a good laugh over this and Alex promised that he would be careful not to do so when Florence was around.

John got on Queen and started home. He was real pleased with the trade. And what was a few loads of wood. He would be clearing trees just across from Alex's place and he could only get a dollar a load if he hauled them all the way to town. He gave Queen a kick in the ribs so they could get home and tell Florence about the trade and also she would have to make another sack of food for Alex.

There was no road work within close range this summer so John cut a lot of hay back in the hills by the swamps. He would have enough to last all winter. He spent time pulling stumps and burning them up. This was in the area where he had cut wood the winter before. This area was below the creek and next to the road that went to Pathlow on the south side of his land. It looked like there was about twenty acres that could be cleared and broken. He had a lot of trees to cut and stumps to pull and burn but the area did not seem to have too many rocks and the soil was good.

Florence did well with the berry picking and canning, even Helen helped with the picking on the lower bushes. She could not reach the Saskatoons, Choke Cherries and the Cranberries. Sometimes she would eat more than she picked. She was easier to keep track of now as she was always chattering about something and Florence could hear where she was.

John got work with the harvest and took grain instead of money. With the hay crop and all they should have a good winter. He kept cutting wood and clearing land right up until Christmas time The only break was when he and Bart did their butchering.

John did not like the butchering this year as it was his turn to kill a beef and it was poor old Lightning that got slaughtered. Everyone was quiet for a few days as he had been their first calf. Florence had said that they should have traded him for another steer and then when they had beef to eat they would not have felt so bad.

They had their regular get together on November the eleventh. And plans were made for Christmas and New Years with the Fords.

One cold night when Helen had been put to bed and John and Florence were sitting by the heater reading with a coal oil lamp between them. John put down his western book that Alex had given him and said to Florence.

"Well Florence this half of the year was sure a lot better than the first half. We have got a good team again. We have picked up some equipment. There is enough hay to last the winter. We have a good supply of food and with the fish that we traded some chickens for at St. Brieux we will have a change of diet from pork and beef."

"Yes", Florence replied. "With chickens, fresh eggs and the odd rooster to eat we are doing well. Selling butter to Alex once in a while helps out some. With a lot of hard work we will make a homestead out of this place yet."

"Oh we can't forget the work that you do and the extra money we get from your efforts. And you know with a bit of luck we may get enough land broken next to put in a crop the following year. You know with getting a dollar a load for the trees that I am cutting we will also be a few dollars ahead by spring."

With this they picked up the light and went upstairs to bed. This had been a good last half of the year and they were both thankful.

Books To Follow

Saskatchewan Homestead
Book Two. 1924-1931.

Saskatchewan Homestead
Book Three. 1932-1939.

Saskatchewan Homestead
Book Four. 1939-1946.

Growing Up On A
Saskatchewan Homestead
Book Five. 1931-1946.

ISBN 141206886-X

9 781412 068864